EKTACHROME 400 Film (Daylight)—4 sec f/8 (Film and exposure data for the illustrations in this book will be given wherever possible. Unless otherwise stated, the ASA value of the film mentioned will be the same as the number in the film name.)

CONTENTS

Tungsten and fluorescent light

Existing-light photography will open new horizons for you. Using a high-speed film in a camera with a fast lens, you can take pictures virtually anywhere—under almost any lighting conditions—without using additional flash or photolamp lighting. Picture-taking by existing light is convenient and such pictures look more natural, because they include only the lighting that already exists on the scene.

This book will introduce you to the fascinating world of existing-light photography. You'll learn what film to use and how to set your camera for many lighting situations. An abundance of good pictures will give you ideas of what to photograph, and an exposure table lists color and black-and-white films with the exposures for a wide variety of lighting conditions. Information on push-processing describes how to take pictures by using less exposure than the lighting conditions would allow if your film were processed normally.

This book will help you take better existing-light pictures and get more enjoyment from the fascinating hobby of photography.

Fluorescent light

ADVENTURES IN
EXISTING-LIGHT PHOTOGRAPHY

It's easy to take colorful and interesting pictures like these by existing light. All you need is a high-speed film and an *adjustable or automatic camera* with a *fast* lens—*f*/2.8 or faster. If you use an automatic camera, it should have a sensitive exposure meter.

When your friends see your finished pictures, chances are that they'll want to know your technique (they may even ask to borrow this book), so read on for some good ideas in picture-taking. Notice the variety of existing-light situations shown on surrounding pages—there is an infinite number of subject/lighting combinations.

Direct sunlight

Daylight

Daylight and tungsten light

Tungsten light and twilight

1
GETTING STARTED IN EXISTING-LIGHT PHOTOGRAPHY

WHAT IS EXISTING LIGHT?

Existing or available light by our definition* includes artificial light which naturally exists in the scene, daylight indoors, and twilight outdoors. It's any light that happens to be on the scene—from table and floor lamps, ceiling fixtures, fluorescent lamps, spotlights, candles, and fireplaces. Existing light is what you find in homes, schools, museums, churches, restaurants, stage shows, and auditoriums. Outdoor scenes at twilight or after dark are considered to be existing-light situations. For the purposes of this book, existing light is characterized by lower light levels than you would encounter in daylight outdoors.

---

*Strictly speaking, existing light covers *all* lighting—from moonlight to sunshine at noon. We're going to limit existing light to mean dim situations that require considerably more exposure than subjects frontlighted by sunshine.

Advantages of Existing-Light Picture-Taking

Your existing-light pictures look realistic because you haven't altered the illumination in the scene. Even a skillfully lighted flash or photolamp picture may appear contrived when compared with a similar existing-light picture.

An existing-light photographer can take pictures that aren't possible with other lighting techniques. Flash may not be appropriate during a wedding ceremony in a church or during a stage show. Flash would disturb the proceedings and might not carry far enough to light your subject. Fortunately, such scenes are often well lighted so you can photograph them with the existing light.

When the sun goes down, many scenic attractions become wonderlands of light. You can make striking pictures of many buildings and monuments around the world that are well illuminated at night. Sparkling fountains reflect a rainbow of colored lights after dark. Even street scenes in your own town or city, which may look rather ordinary during the day, become exciting subjects after sunset. These subjects are too far away for flash, but you can easily photograph them by existing light because camera-to-subject distance won't affect your exposure.

Existing-light picture-taking is inexpensive and convenient. Without lighting accessories, you can concentrate on your subjects, and you have greater freedom of movement. Speaking of subjects, people will really appreciate your existing-light approach because they won't be disturbed by bright photolamps or flashes from flashbulbs. In fact, they may not even notice you're taking pictures—you'll get an added bonus with relaxed, candid expressions.

With the magic of existing-light photography you can easily capture exciting scenes like this.

EQUIPMENT AND FILM

High-speed films and fast (wide-aperture) lenses allow a handheld camera (no tripod) for most scenes and provide the capability for making candid pictures in existing light. Finally, the saying "If you can see it, you can photograph it" is a reality.

Camera Requirements

If you have an adjustable or automatic camera that has a sensitive exposure meter and an $f/2.8$ or faster lens, you're all set for taking many existing-light pictures. If your camera lens is slower, you can still explore the world of existing-light picture-taking, but you'll sometimes need your three-legged friend the tripod to make time exposures. If your camera doesn't have a built-in exposure meter, a separate sensitive meter will be a big help in determining the correct exposure.

Films for Existing-Light Picture-Taking

For greatest versatility in most existing-light situations, try a high-speed film like KODACOLOR 400 Film* for color prints; KODAK EKTACHROME 400 Film (Daylight), KODAK EKTACHROME 200 Film (Daylight), or KODAK EKTACHROME 160 Film (Tungsten) for color slides; or KODAK TRI-X Pan Film for black-and-white prints. A special processing service offered by Kodak is a real boon to the existing-light photographer. When you purchase the KODAK Special Processing Envelope, ESP-1, available from photo dealers, Kodak will push-process your EKTACHROME 400, 200, or 160 Films in the 135 and 120 sizes to 2 times normal speed. See page 71 for information on special processing.

Each color film is recommended for use with a specific type of light. To obtain the most pleasing color rendition in your pictures, expose the film under the lighting conditions recommended by the manufacturer. For example, KODAK EKTACHROME 200 Film (Daylight) is balanced for daylight illumination. When you expose this film by tungsten lighting (without a light-balancing filter), the resulting pictures will look warm (yellow-red). KODAK EKTACHROME 160 Film (Tungsten) is designed for 3200 K tungsten illumination. This film produces pleasing results under most existing tungsten light (regular light bulbs or tungsten floodlights). For taking pictures under fluorescent illumination, Daylight film is best, although your results still can appear greenish. Outdoors at night you can use either film.

KODACOLOR 400 Film, although balanced for daylight, provides pleasing and natural-appearing pictures with nearly any illumination, natural or artificial.

The tables on pages 67 and 74 will help you select the best film for your existing-light pictures. Chapter 6 discusses films for existing-light photography in more detail.

SOME IMPORTANT POINTS TO REMEMBER

- Take pictures by existing light for natural expressions and realism.
- Use a camera with a fast lens, $f/2.8$ or faster, and a high-speed film for handheld pictures.
- If your camera has a slower lens, use a tripod to make time exposures.
- For color pictures, use Daylight color film with daylight or fluorescent illumination; use Tungsten film for tungsten illumination. For color pictures outdoors at night you can use either film.

*Equivalents can be used for the Kodak products mentioned.

Tungsten light. EKTACHROME 160 Film (Tungsten)—⅛ sec f/5.6

2
TAKING EXISTING-LIGHT PICTURES AT HOME

PICTURE-TAKING OPPORTUNITIES

Many of your best picture-taking opportunities occur at home. Special occasions such as birthdays, anniversaries, and holidays present excellent opportunities for existing-light pictures. There are events going on every day in your home that are special, too. For example, when the baby is bathing or the children are playing, you can take pictures of them as they really are. They may not even notice you and your camera, so you'll be able to capture natural expressions. In years to come, your everyday photos may be the ones you'll treasure most because they'll show your family and friends natural and unposed, doing the things they enjoy most.

People at play, people at work, or people at ease make interesting existing-light subjects.

NORM KERR

The soft, diffuse quality of daylight indoors is excellent for informal portraits. KODACOLOR 400 Film— 1/30 sec f/5.6

JEANNETTE KLUTE

HOME LIGHTING

Indoor scenes at home with existing daylight or artificial light are relatively dim compared with daylight outdoors. Because the human eye is very adaptable to a large range of lighting conditions, many people are not aware of the low-light levels in the home. At night, with all the lights turned on, the average living room with a light-colored ceiling has only about 1/800 as much light as you'll find outdoors in sunlight. Under these dim lighting conditions, a high-speed film and a camera with a fast lens are a must for taking *handheld* pictures.

JOHN VAETH

Photograph the thrill of birthdays, holidays, and everyday activities in your home by existing light.

Daylight Indoors

You can take very pleasing pictures with daylight coming through the windows of your home, and you don't have to concern yourself with the weather. The lighting on overcast days is excellent for informal portraits indoors. It has a soft, diffuse quality which is flattering for pictures of people. It's even better when there is snow on the ground, since this acts as a reflector.

Existing daylight coming through the windows is usually brighter than the artificial light in the home. Take advantage of the light from the windows by opening all the drapes or curtains. This raises the light level in the room, making it easier to get enough exposure, and makes the lighting more even and less contrasty. (You'll be able to record more detail in bright areas and shadow areas.)

On sunny days the areas in the room that are *not* in direct sunlight are usually best for picture-taking. The lighting is less contrasty and is similar to the diffuse lighting on overcast days. But you can also get some good pictures when your subject is in direct sunlight near a window. Turn your subject's face toward the win-

JOHN MENIHAN

Facing this violin student into the sun could have produced a squinting expression. Facing away from the window, she can concentrate on the music, relax her expression, and allow reflected light from the sheet music to raise the light level on her face. Notice how the photographer moved in close to reduce window area in the picture. KODAK EKTACHROME 200 Film (Daylight)— 1/125 sec f/4

BOB CLEMENS

You may get a semisilhouette when a bright window is directly behind your subject.
If you set your exposure for the scene, your center of interest will be underexposed and the window will be correctly exposed.

On the other hand, if you expose for your subject, the window will be overexposed, taking some of the attention from the center of interest.

A good solution is to locate your subject a few feet away from the window. Find a camera angle that excludes the window but allows window light to illuminate your subject's face. EKTACHROME 200 Film (Daylight)—1/30 sec f/4

dow, or select a camera angle that includes a minimum of shadow area. The bright sunlight lets you use higher shutter speeds and smaller lens openings or a slower-speed film than you can use for most other existing-light pictures.

A subject in front of a bright window will photograph as a silhouette. Avoid this silhouette effect by shooting from a position beside the window or by exposing for the shadow side of the subject. If there are no other windows in the room to help lighten the shadows, try to stand so that the window is behind you.

Your reflected-light exposure meter or automatic camera can be misled by a bright window included in the scene. Either make a close-up meter reading of the subject or select a camera angle that doesn't include the window in the picture. Determining exposure is discussed in Chapter 4.

You can also reduce contrast by using a reflector, such as a piece of white cloth, white cardboard, or crumpled aluminum foil, to fill in the shadows. Place the reflector on the shadow side of your subject so that the reflector is facing the window that provides most of the light. Make sure the reflector is far enough away so that it's not included in the picture. While this may not be pure existing light, you can forgive yourself for stretching the truth a little when it helps you improve your final result.

On clear days, when you're taking pictures in an area of the room that is not in direct sunlight, but where the blue sky is providing most of the light, try a skylight filter (No. 1A) to reduce bluishness in your color slides. This filter does not require any increase in exposure.

White ceiling and walls provided enough reflected light to brighten the shadows on the indoor gardener's face.

You can fill in shadows on a face illuminated from the side with reflections from a large white card or projection screen.
EKTACHROME 200 Film (Daylight)—
1/30 sec f/4

Natural reflectors, in this case a newspaper, can also help provide even illumination.
KODACOLOR 400 Film—1/60 sec f/4

Artificial Lighting

Artificial lighting at home is usually contrasty because it includes brightly lighted areas around lamps and comparatively darker areas in the other parts of the room. Turning on *all the lights* in the room reduces the contrast and raises the light level so that you may have enough light to handhold your camera and obtain proper exposure. (See the exposure table on page 54.) House lamps with translucent shades are best for most existing-light pictures. Pole lamps or gooseneck lamps, which give more directional light, are handy to use when you want direct light on your subject or want a spotlight effect in the scene.

Most household lamps have tungsten light bulbs. Use a color film designed for tungsten light to get pleasing color rendition in your pictures. In rooms illuminated by fluorescent light, use Daylight color film without a filter. Recommendations for using color films with these and other light sources are given in Chapter 6.

Since black-and-white film doesn't record the color of the light in the scene, you can use it with any kind of lighting.

It's difficult to judge by eye the differences in the amounts of light from one scene to another in your home. Use an exposure meter or an automatic camera to determine exposure. A lighted lamp included in the scene may mislead your reflected-light meter, so take a close-up reading of the principal subject, *excluding* the lamp.

Lighting Direction. When you're taking pictures of a person or a pet, illuminate the front or side of the face. When you need more light, photograph your subject near a lamp. Turning on all the other lights in the room will help brighten the shadows. You can also use a reflector, as described under **Daylight Indoors.**

BOB CLEMENS

A lighted lamp in the background put the subject's face in shadow. Moving the camera captured more pleasing lighting on the activity in progress. EKTACHROME 160 Film (Tungsten)—1/60 sec f/4 ↓ 5.6

JOHN MENIHAN

Turning on all the room lights helps to even the illumination and provides more light for taking the picture. EKTACHROME 160 Film (Tungsten)—1/30 sec f/2.8

14

Adding Bounce Lighting

You can minimize the contrast of the lighting and increase the amount of light in the room by bouncing fill light off a white ceiling. Adding bounce light means you won't be making true existing-light pictures. But this additional light can improve the existing light without spoiling its natural appearance. The extra light may also let you use a shutter speed fast enough to handhold your camera when otherwise you might have to use a tripod. If you're using a high-speed film, this added light may allow you to use a smaller lens opening for increased depth of field. (For more on depth of field, see page 60.) Since bounce light makes the lighting more uniform, you can often use one exposure setting to photograph your subject as he or she moves around the room in the general vicinity of the bounce light. This is especially convenient for photographing active children.

Take color pictures with bounce lighting in a room that has a white or light, neutral-colored ceiling, because a colored ceiling will reflect its color onto your subject. For black-and-white pictures, the color of the ceiling is unimportant, although a lighter color will reflect more illumination.

A movie light held by an assistant will provide a convenient method for bounce lighting. A reflector photolamp in a clamp-on light socket also makes a versatile bounce light. Photo stores sell both the lamps and the clamping devices. Clamp the photolamp to the back of a chair, the edge of a door, a tripod, or anything that's handy. In a pinch, you can put a reflector photolamp into almost any light socket that you can aim at the ceiling. Pole lamps or gooseneck lamps can serve the purpose. Beware of lamps with shades as hot photolamps can ruin them.

BOB CLEMENS

Bounce-lighting from a photolamp created even illumination in the room and increased the light level. EKTACHROME 160 Film (Tungsten)—1/30 sec f/2.8

15

SUGGESTED EXPOSURES FOR
BOUNCE LIGHTING PLUS ROOM LIGHTS

KODAK Film	ASA Film Speed	Shutter Speed	Lens Opening
For Color Prints			
KODACOLOR 400	400	$^1/_{60}$ sec	f/4
KODACOLOR II	100	$^1/_{30}$ sec	f/2.8
For Color Slides			
EKTACHROME 400 (Daylight)	400*	$^1/_{60}$ sec	f/4
	125 with No. 80B filter	$^1/_{30}$ sec	f/2.8
	800*†	$^1/_{60}$ sec	f/5.6
	250† with No. 80B filter	$^1/_{60}$ sec	f/2.8
EKTACHROME 200 (Daylight)	200*	$^1/_{30}$ sec	f/4
	400*†	$^1/_{60}$ sec	f/4
	125† with No. 80B filter	$^1/_{30}$ sec	f/2.8
EKTACHROME 160 (Tungsten)	160	$^1/_{30}$ sec	f/2.8 ↓ 4
	320†	$^1/_{30}$ sec	f/4 ↓ 5.6
KODACHROME 64 (Daylight) EKTACHROME 64 (Daylight)	64*	$^1/_{30}$ sec	f/2
For Black-and-White Prints			
TRI-X Pan	400	$^1/_{60}$ sec	f/4
VERICHROME Pan PLUS-X Pan	125	$^1/_{30}$ sec	f/2.8

Note: The ↓ symbol indicates the lens opening halfway between the two f-numbers.

*Pictures taken with daylight film and no filter will look yellow-red.
†With ESP-1 Processing—sizes 135 and 120.

Place the lamp approximately 3 to 5 feet from the ceiling near the area where you want to take pictures. Aim the lamp so that the light will strike the ceiling between your camera and the subject. Don't let direct light from the photolamp illuminate your subject.

Bounce light and the room lighting together can provide about 6 times as much light as you would have with room lighting alone. (See the bounce-light exposure table.) Use an automatic camera or an exposure meter to get the right exposure. If you don't have either one, use the table above as a guide to exposure. The exposures in this table are based on the use of a 625 to 650-watt tungsten-halogen movie light or a 650-watt sealed-beam movie light, aimed at a white ceiling. These same exposures apply to a three-lamp movie light equipped with 300- or 375-watt reflector photolamps. If you use two 300- or 375-watt reflector photolamps, try a lens opening ½ stop larger than that shown in the table. For one 300- or 375-watt reflector photolamp, use a lens opening 1 stop larger than the table indicates.

WARNING: Read the manufacturer's instructions before using any movie light.

JOHN FISH

The dim room lighting was assisted by a bare 100-watt bulb, allowing the photographer to make a handheld exposure. KODACOLOR 400 Film— 1/60 sec f/1.4

JOHN MENIHAN

It's easy to capture candid expressions when party guests are absorbed in an activity.

BOB ROWE

JEANNETTE KLUTE

To take handheld pictures in average home lighting, you need a fast lens and a high-speed film. KODACOLOR 400 Film—1/30 sec f/2.8 ↓ 4

PHOTOGRAPHING YOUR TELEVISION SCREEN

It's fun to take pictures of the images on your television screen. Television gives you the opportunity to see many important events right in your own home. Political conventions, the inauguration of the President, the Olympics, and the Academy Award presentations are just a few of the many shows on television that you may want to photograph. You can use either color or black-and-white film to take pictures of color or black-and-white television images.

You'll get the best quality in your photographs when you adjust your set so that the contrast of the television picture is slightly lower than normal. Set the brightness control so that both the highlight and shadow areas of the TV image show detail. Adjust the color controls on a color set for a pleasing color picture on the screen. Move close until the television screen fills the picture area in your camera viewfinder. You may want to use a close-up lens if the screen is small.

If your camera is a single-lens reflex with through-the-lens viewing, you can see exactly what you'll get in close-up pictures. But if the viewfinder on your camera is separate and offset from the lens, it may not show you exactly what you'll get. (See your camera manual.) To center the TV screen on your film with a camera of this type, tip the camera slightly in the direction of the viewfinder to take the picture.

You will need a tripod for shutter speeds slower than 1/30 second. (See **Shutter Speed and Exposure**.)

CAROLINE GRIMES

It's easy to photograph the image on your TV screen. Both: EKTACHROME 200 Film (Daylight)—⅛ sec f/4 ↓ 5.6

SUGGESTED CAMERA SETTINGS
FOR PICTURES OF TELEVISION IMAGES

KODAK Film	Color Television Set		Black-and-White Television Set	
	Focal-Plane Shutter	Leaf Shutter	Focal-Plane Shutter	Leaf Shutter
VERICHROME Pan PLUS-X Pan	$^1/_8$ sec f/5.6	$^1/_{30}$ sec f/2.8	$^1/_8$ sec f/8	$^1/_{30}$ sec f/4
TRI-X Pan	$^1/_8$ sec f/8 ↓ 11	$^1/_{30}$ sec f/4 ↓5.6	$^1/_8$ sec f/11 ↓ 16	$^1/_{30}$ sec f/5.6 ↓ 8
KODACHROME 64 (Daylight)* EKTACHROME 64 (Daylight)* KODACOLOR II*	$^1/_8$ sec. f/2.8	$^1/_8$ sec f/2.8 or $^1/_{15}$ sec f/2	$^1/_8$ sec f/2.8	$^1/_8$ sec f/2.8 or $^1/_{15}$ sec f/2
EKTACHROME 200 (Daylight)* —with normal processing	$^1/_8$ sec f/5.6	$^1/_{30}$ sec f/2.8	$^1/_8$ sec f/5.6	$^1/_{30}$ sec f/2.8
EKTACHROME 400 (Daylight)* KODACOLOR 400* EKTACHROME 200 (Daylight)* —with ESP-1 Processing for a speed of ASA 400	$^1/_8$ sec f/8	$^1/_{30}$ sec f/4	$^1/_8$ sec f/8	$^1/_{30}$ sec f/4
EKTACHROME 400 (Daylight)* —with ESP-1 Processing for a speed of ASA 800	$^1/_8$ sec f/11	$^1/_{30}$ sec f/5.6	$^1/_8$ sec f/11	$^1/_{30}$ sec f/5.6

Note: The ↓ symbol indicates the lens opening halfway between the two f-numbers.

Important: With focal-plane shutters, use a shutter speed of $^1/_8$ second or slower. With leaf shutters, use a shutter speed of $^1/_{30}$ second or slower. These precautions are necessary to prevent dark streaks in your pictures.

*Pictures of color television taken without a filter will look somewhat blue-green. With the color films in the table you can use a KODAK Color Compensating Filter CC40R over your camera lens to help bring out the reds in your pictures. Increase the exposure suggested in the table by 1 stop. Since KODACOLOR 400 Film does not require a filter for this application, the use of a CC40R filter is not recommended.

Room Lighting

Avoid reflections on the face of the television tube. To help eliminate reflections, turn off most or all of the room lights. Don't use flash or photolamps to photograph television images. As flash is much brighter than the TV image, your pictures would show a blank television screen.

Shutter Speed and Exposure

The television image is formed by a moving electron beam which takes 1/30 second to make a complete picture on the screen. You must use a shutter speed of 1/8 second or slower to record at least one complete picture cycle with a focal-plane shutter. (Use 1/30 second or slower with other shutters. Read your camera instruction manual if you're not sure of your kind of shutter.)

To get sharp pictures with these slow shutter speeds, try to take the picture when the subject on the screen is not moving.

You can determine exposure by holding a reflected-light exposure meter close enough to the screen so that it reads only the TV image. Hold the meter so that it reads approximately equal parts of light and dark

If you use a shutter speed faster than ⅛ second with a focal-plane shutter, you'll get a dark band across your picture. EKTACHROME 400 Film (Daylight)—left ⅛ sec f/8; right 1/125 sec f/2

areas of the TV picture. If you are using a camera with a built-in meter, fill the picture area with the TV screen so that the meter reads only the screen. If your camera is too far away from the TV screen, the exposure meter reads too much of the dark area surrounding the TV image, resulting in overexposure on your film. If you don't have an exposure meter, you can use the table on page 20 as an exposure guide.

Many television programs are copyrighted. Eastman Kodak Company undertakes no responsibility concerning any copyright matters which may be involved in photographing television images. The mere taking of pictures of a television program might be deemed a violation of the copyright, and responsibility for complying with the copyright requirements must remain with the person taking the photograph.

SOME IMPORTANT POINTS TO REMEMBER

- Indoor lighting on overcast days is very flattering for pictures of people.
- Open all the drapes in the room for existing-daylight pictures. For picture-taking at night, turn on all the lights in the room.
- Photograph your subject so that window light or household lamps are lighting the side or front of the face. Try to avoid photographing your subject with a bright window or a lighted lamp directly behind.
- Select camera angles that show a minimum of shadow on your subject.
- If you are using a reflected-light exposure meter, make a close-up meter reading of your subject when the scene includes a bright window or a lighted lamp which may mislead the meter.
- Use a reflector or bounce lighting to brighten deep shadows and reduce lighting contrast.
- You can take pictures of your television screen. With focal-plane shutters, use 1/8 second or slower; with leaf shutters, use a shutter speed of 1/30 second or slower.

21

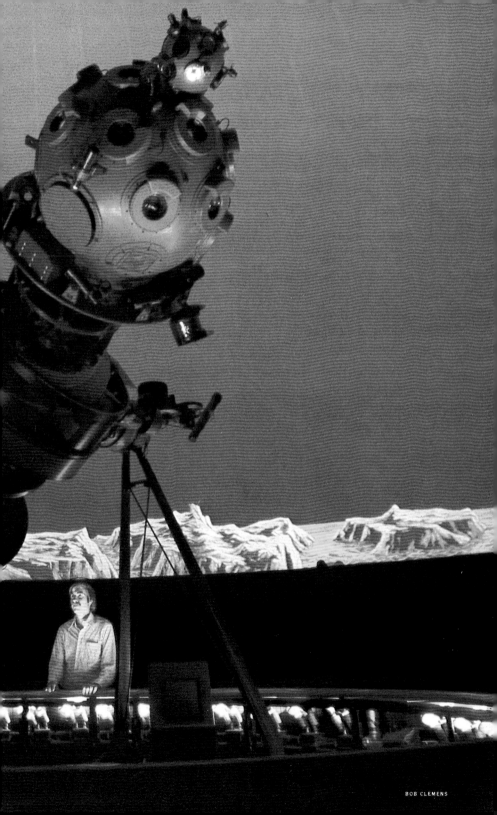

3
TAKING EXISTING-LIGHT PICTURES IN PUBLIC PLACES

Almost everywhere you go around a town or city, you will find possibilities for existing-light pictures. You can capture the colorful lights of holiday displays in your own neighborhood, the myriad neon signs in a downtown street scene, and the fantasy atmosphere of fairs and carnivals. Indoors you'll find exotic displays and dioramas in museums, lighted fountains in shopping malls, and beautiful flowers in bloom the year round in botanical gardens and conservatories.

When you go on a trip, there will be all kinds of opportunities for existing-light pictures. If you take pictures only outdoors in the daytime, you'll miss the chance to capture some of the most interesting sights on your tour. Many of the sights you'll see are indoors, and pictures you take by existing light will show realistic, natural-looking interiors. Many places take on an entirely different look at night when the lights come on. Creative lighting plays an important role on much architecture. You'll find that night scenes offer excellent pictorial possibilities and night pictures will add a change of pace to your travel pictures.

When you're sitting in the grandstand at a sports event, the action is too far away for flash pictures. But existing-light photography allows you to make dramatic pictures of sporting events outdoors at night and indoors any time.

Let's examine the existing-light picture possibilities that we might find in a variety of public places.

CAROLINE GRIMES

The sky will appear a deep blue against illuminated buildings in pictures taken at twilight. Reflections in the water add foreground interest to this Chicago scene. KODACOLOR 400 Film—1/30 sec f/2.8

Include a night view such as this and a daytime picture of the same subject for a dramatic comparison in your travel pictures.

To complete a picture story during your travels, take pictures of interesting exhibits indoors. It's polite to ask permission first. KODACOLOR 400 Film—1/30 sec f/2.8

Outdoor scenes at dusk, like this New York skyline, are easy to photograph by existing light.

OUTDOOR SCENES AT NIGHT

Outdoor night scenes usually include large areas of darkness pierced by spots of light from signs, streetlights, and buildings. Pictures of such scenes are easy to take because you can get good results anywhere in a fairly wide range of exposures. Short exposures emphasize the bright areas by preserving the detail while the shadows go dark. Long exposures show more detail in the shadows and reduce detail in the brightest areas.

The large dark areas in many night scenes make it difficult to use an exposure meter from the camera position. You can make a close-up meter reading of the important areas in your picture or use the exposure recommended in the table on pages 54-56. When you're photographing evenly illuminated subjects, such as flood-lighted buildings, statues, and store windows, try to get close enough to take an exposure-meter reading.

When you go outdoors for night pictures, take a small flashlight to help you make camera settings in the dark.

For outdoor picture-taking at night, you can choose either Daylight film or Tungsten film. This is a matter of personal taste. Pictures taken on Tungsten film may look more natural, while pictures taken on Daylight film will have a warmer (more yellow-red) appearance. Both films produce pleasing results.

An excellent time to take pictures of street scenes, floodlighted buildings, city skylines, and other outdoor night subjects is at twilight, just before complete darkness. Your pictures will show a rich color in the sky instead of just black. Lights are usually turned on at dusk, before the sky becomes completely dark. While there is still some light in the sky (about 10 minutes after sunset), you can make pictures at 1/60 second at f/5.6 on

Pictures of night scenes recorded on Tungsten film may appear more natural, while those on Daylight film have a warmer, more yellow-red appearance. Both types of film produce pleasing results. Top EKTACHROME 160 Film (Tungsten)— 1/30 sec f/2.8 ↓ 4. Bottom EKTACHROME 200 Film (Daylight)—1/30 sec f/2.8 ↓ 4

KODAK EKTACHROME 400 Film (Daylight). Since lighting conditions are so variable at this time of day, you will want to bracket your exposure. (Bracketing exposures is explained on page 53.)

Street Scenes

Signs in theatre, nightclub, or shopping districts make brightly colored subjects for your pictures. The best time to take pictures in business districts is on shopping nights when the stores are open, because more buildings are lighted. An excellent time to take these pictures is during or just after a rain. The lights will produce a myriad of colorful reflections on the wet pavement, adding interest to otherwise black, empty areas of your pictures. For a colorful abstraction, move close to a rain puddle so that the reflections become the main subject for your picture.

If your camera permits double exposures, you can make several exposures of different neon signs on the *same frame of film.* By placing the signs in different locations on the film, you can create an unusual montage. Make a mental note of the placement of the sign for each exposure so that you will create a pleasing design. Check the instruction manual for your camera to see whether you can use this technique.

Store windows often have elaborate and colorful displays strengthened by dramatic lighting. Take a close-up meter reading through the window glass and try to select a camera angle that minimizes distracting reflections from the window.

When you go window-shopping for colorful displays with your camera, look for an angle that will avoid reflections on the glass. KODACOLOR 400 Film—1/60 sec f/4

27

Reflections of colored lights on water-soaked pavement create interesting splashes of color. KODACOLOR 400 Film— 1/60 sec f/2.8

JOHN FISH

BYRON TOBIAS, KINSA*

Move in close to make photographic abstractions from wet-street reflections.

*Courtesy Kodak International Newspaper Snapshot Awards.

HERB JONES

By making several exposures on the same frame of film or by using a multiple lens attachment, you can create a unique montage with bright, multicolored signs.
Left KODACOLOR 400 Film—1/125 sec f/4
Right KODACHROME 64 Film—1/60 sec f/4

MARTIN FOLB

Holiday Lights Outdoors

Around the holiday season, many neighborhoods, downtown streets, and shopping centers are ablaze with color. Buildings with outdoor holiday lights make good subjects for color pictures. If there is snow on the ground, you can get pictorial effects by including the reflections of the colored lights on the snow. On very cold nights, keep your camera tucked inside your coat until you're ready to take pictures. Cold weather may make some shutters sluggish.

Floodlighted Buildings, Fountains, and Statues

Many buildings, fountains, and statues look rather ordinary in the daytime, but at night they are often beautifully lighted. Try framing such subjects with an object like a tree branch in the foreground. You can make interesting comparison pictures by shooting the same buildings or fountains during the day and again at night.

CAROLINE GRIMES

Photograph the lighting display at your home for an ideal picture for next year's holiday greeting card. The exposure on EKTACHROME 160 Film (Tungsten) would be ¼ sec f/1.7.

HERB FORCE

You can get some spectacular pictures of Niagara Falls at night when the falls are illuminated by colored lights. Put your camera onto a tripod and make a time exposure. (See the exposure table on page 55.) Shield your camera and lens from the spray and mist always present around the falls. This once-in-a-lifetime photo with fireworks was taken during a Bicentennial celebration.

If you take sports pictures outdoors at night during those brief moments when the players are almost motionless, you can use a slower shutter speed than you would normally need for stopping action. Both: KODACOLOR 400 Film—1/125 sec f/1.8

Halftime festivity helps to complete your story of the game. KODACOLOR 400 Film—1/60 sec f/1.8

Outdoor Sporting Events at Night

Night sports that are well lighted provide excellent subjects for existing-light pictures. Outdoor events may be illuminated with tungsten light. Many modern stadiums have mercury-vapor lamps, which have a blue-green appearance when compared with tungsten lamps. Even if you use Daylight film with mercury-vapor lighting, your pictures will appear blue-green because the lights are deficient in red.

When possible, use a very high-speed film so that you can use shutter speeds fast enough to stop some action. See the exposure table on page 55. Don't worry if you can't freeze the action completely. Motion that's a bit blurred gives pictures a feeling of action. Stopping action is discussed in greater detail under **Indoor Sports,** page 41.

Fairs and Amusement Parks

Fairs and amusement parks become a wonderland of colored lights at night. The festive outdoor lighting that you'll find in these places is superb for existing-light pictures. You can take handheld pictures of lighted buildings, the midway, and the many colorful signs. Since lighting is such an important part of modern living, world's fairs and similar expositions display the latest lighting innovations. It's truly a world of color for your camera.

KEITH BOAS

Bright colors and interesting shapes in amusement parks at sundown and at night provide many opportunities for existing-light pictures. Top EKTACHROME 64 Film—1/250 sec f/5.6. Bottom KODACOLOR 400 Film—½ sec f/2.8

KEITH BOAS

31

Handholding your camera for a time exposure of fireworks gives a brush-stroke appearance to the light trails. KODACOLOR II Film—ASA 100; 2 sec f/8; 135 mm lens on a 35 mm camera

Including a lighted or silhouetted subject in your fireworks pictures adds extra interest.

Fireworks and Lightning

Fireworks displays are easy and fun to photograph. You'll get the best pictures of aerial displays if you put your camera onto a tripod and capture several bursts in the same picture by making a time exposure. Focus your camera on infinity, and aim it in the direction of the display. Exposure is not critical. A larger lens opening will make the lines in the burst thicker and lighter; a smaller lens opening will make the lines thinner and darker. Set the lens opening on your camera according to the exposure table on page 55, and with the shutter set on BULB or TIME, keep the shutter open for several bursts.

If you don't have a tripod for making time exposures, you can get successful results by handholding your camera and using an exposure of 1/30 second at f/2 on KODAK EKTACHROME 64 Film (Daylight). Take your pictures when the fireworks bursts are at their fullest.

Nature offers spectacular fireworks of her own.

RAY ATKESON

You can add interest and a feeling of depth to your fireworks pictures by including lighted buildings, a city sky-line, lights reflected in water, or sil-houettes of objects in the foreground. If you have a telephoto lens for your camera, use it to take close-up pic-tures of fireworks displays.

Since fireworks displays on the ground last several seconds or longer and don't move across the scene, you can use shorter exposure times. For ground displays you don't need a tri-pod; you can take pictures by hand-holding your camera and using a shut-ter speed of 1/30 second. (See the ex-posure table on page 55.)

Taking pictures of lightning is sim-ilar to photographing fireworks, ex-cept that you don't know exactly when or where it will strike. To capture the lightning in your pictures, put your camera onto a tripod and hold the shutter open for one or more flashes. Since you and your tripod would be likely targets for lightning, be very careful to avoid open spaces out-doors. Take your pictures from inside a building through an open window or from some other location (not under a tree) that offers protection.

Because you don't know exactly when or where the lightning will streak across the sky, use a normal or wide-angle lens on your camera. This will increase your chances of having your camera aimed in the right direction, because these lenses include more of the sky than a telephoto lens does. You may have to hold the shutter open for quite some time, so it's best to take pictures of lightning away from city lights and car lights. If there are no bright lights around, you can hold the shutter open for a minute or two when necessary, until the lightning streaks across the sky. If a car goes by, cover your camera lens temporarily with an object such as a hat so that the car lights don't spoil your picture.

Museum lighting is designed to enhance the objects on display. With high-speed film you can get excellent pictures. EKTACHROME 400 Film (Daylight)—1/30 sec f/3.5

INDOOR OPPORTUNITIES FOR EXISTING-LIGHT PICTURES

Museums and Galleries

Museums, art galleries, and other public buildings can provide many subjects for existing-light pictures. Some museums offer a great variety of unusual sights, from giant models of prehistoric animals to priceless gems in exquisite settings. The lighting is often arranged to enhance the items on display. Take advantage of this artful lighting when you take pictures.

The elaborate dioramas in many museums make especially good subjects for existing-light pictures. Dioramas usually have painted backgrounds, so use a large lens opening to throw the background slightly out of focus and make the scene appear more realistic.

Museums and art galleries sometimes have fluorescent lights or skylight windows that let in daylight illumination, so use Daylight film for best results under these lighting conditions.

Some museums and galleries don't allow picture-taking, although these restrictions aren't too common. Others do not permit the use of tripods or flash units but do permit you to hand-hold your camera for taking pictures by existing light. It's a good idea to check with the museum personnel before taking pictures. You may even want to telephone the museum ahead of time.

KODACOLOR 400 Film—1/60 sec f/2

When you photograph glassware in a window, move in close and try an exposure 1 stop greater than you would use for the outdoor lighting conditions. KODAK EKTACHROME 64 Film (Daylight)—1/125 sec f/4

Colonial Williamsburg, Virginia. The exposure for the lighting in this scene would be 1/60 sec f/4 on KODACOLOR II Film—ASA 100.

JOHN MENIHAN

JOYCE WIDOFF

The beautiful costumes, choreography, and settings of ice shows create a special existing-light magic. Top The Ice Follies on KODACOLOR 400 Film—1/250 sec f/2.8. Bottom The Ice Follies on KODACOLOR 400 Film—1/125 sec f/3.5

Circuses and Ice Shows

Photographing these colorful spectaculars by existing light is a natural because they are well lighted and the subjects are usually too far away for you to use flash. The brilliant costumes and lighting give outstanding results with color film. You will want to get a printed program for the show before you take your seat, to help you plan your picture-taking.

The lighting at circuses and ice shows is provided by two general kinds of light—carbon-arc spotlights and general tungsten lighting. You can use either Daylight or Tungsten film—it's a matter of personal preference. Daylight film gives the best color rendition for acts lighted by carbon-arc spotlights. Pictures of these scenes made on Tungsten film will look somewhat bluish. Since the general, overall lighting that illuminates the arena or ice is usually tungsten, Tungsten film gives the most natural color rendition; Daylight film gives yellow-red results. When colored filters are used over the lights, both types of film will give equally good results. Since you'll probably want to use one kind of color film, you might like to try KODAK EKTACHROME 400 Film (Daylight) for color slides or KODACOLOR 400 Film for color prints.

36

With all the interesting acts at the Shrine or any other circus, you'll find plenty to photograph. In many existing-light situations it's wise to wait for a moment when the action is temporarily halted.

EKTACHROME 200 Film
(Daylight)—1/60 sec f/5.6

JIM DENNIS

EKTACHROME 400 Film
(Daylight)—1/250 sec f/2.8

JIM DENNIS

EKTACHROME 200 Film
(Daylight)—1/60 sec f/5.6

JIM DENNIS

EKTACHROME 400 Film
(Daylight)—ASA 800 with ESP-1
Processing, 1/250 sec f/2.8

CAROLINE GRIMES

Photographing a wedding by existing light lets you take pictures without fear of disturbing the ceremony. KODACOLOR 400 Film—1/125 sec f/4

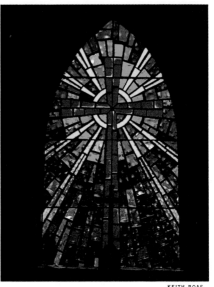

Many churches and other public buildings have stained-glass windows. The rich colors and intricate designs can add variety to your picture collection. Make an exposure-meter reading of the window to determine exposure. KODACOLOR II Film—ASA 100, 1/60 sec f/4

Churches

Many important family events like weddings and baptisms take place in church. Flash is often inappropriate for picture-taking on such occasions. However, you can record these meaningful events by existing light without causing any disturbance. For example, you can get very good pictures of a wedding ceremony from the balcony, where you can be unobtrusive about your picture-taking and can steady your camera on the balcony railing. Take long shots that include much of the church interior, and then use a telephoto lens for close-up views.

During your travels, you may visit churches rich with historical significance or tour creations of modern architecture filled with the promise of the future. Churches make interesting and colorful subject matter for existing-light pictures.

The illumination in churches may be primarily tungsten or daylight, depending on how much light the windows let in and the time of day. Choose the appropriate type of color film for the predominant lighting. After you've taken an overall view of the church interior, move close for pictures showing the detail of the structure, such as intricate carvings and statues.

Stained-glass windows make unusual and extremely colorful picture subjects, too. Photograph them from inside the church with daylight shining through the glass. Move in close to the window to determine your exposure so that the meter reads only the light coming through the window. If you don't have a meter, try an expo-

The architectural beauty of the church is preserved in this existing-light photograph.

sure with the lens opening 3 stops larger than you would use for the outdoor lighting conditions. For example, if the sun is shining on the window, a typical exposure for a film with a speed of ASA 64 is 1/125 second at $f/4$. On a clear day when the sun isn't striking the window, try 1/30 second at $f/2.8$. It's a good idea to bracket your exposure. (See page 53.)

Your Transportation

When you're traveling, take a few pictures of your family inside the car, plane, or train to help build a story sequence for your travel pictures. Daylight coming through the windows provides the best lighting. Use an exposure meter to find the right exposure.

Take your pictures when the ride is smooth, and hold your camera steady to avoid camera movement. Vibration can cause blurred pictures, so don't brace your arms or hands against any part of the vehicle.

School Events

Many school events like plays, parties, graduation ceremonies, and indoor sports contests make good subject matter for your pictures. In the daytime there is usually plenty of light for indoor picture-taking if the school has large windows. At night the light is dimmer, but the overhead lighting is usually sufficient for taking pictures. It's best to use an exposure meter.

Stage lighting in auditoriums is usually provided by tungsten lights. In classrooms, gymnasiums, and swimming pools, the overhead lighting may

BOB OLSON

Activities in a gymnasium or an indoor sports arena are easy to photograph because the lighting is so even. Top KODACOLOR 400 Film—1/60 sec f/2.8. Middle KODACOLOR 400 Film—1/60 sec f/2 ↓ 2.8

JOHN MENIHAN

Capturing life in a schoolroom with existing light is a pleasant assignment. KODACOLOR 400 Film—1/125 sec f/2.8

JOHN MENIHAN

be tungsten, fluorescent, or mercury vapor. In the daytime, daylight is usually combined with the artificial overhead lighting. See pages 65 through 70 for color-film suggestions.

Indoor Sports

High-school and college sports are fun to photograph, particularly if a friend or relative is on the team. Professional sporting events also offer color and action in existing light.

Find out in advance whether the gymnasium lighting is tungsten, fluorescent, or mercury vapor, and take along the appropriate film. To determine exposure, take a close-up meter reading of the gym floor area before the action begins.

To stop the action, use the highest shutter speed that the lighting will allow. You can use higher shutter speeds with high-speed films like KODACOLOR 400 Film, KODAK EKTACHROME 400 Film (Daylight), KODAK TRI-X Pan Film, or KODAK ROYAL-X Pan Film.

There are other action-stopping techniques, too. Look for moments when the action is temporarily halted or slowed—the peak of action. For example, when a basketball player is at the highest point of a jump, there is a split second of suspended action. Snapping the picture at the peak of action freezes the motion on your picture.

The direction of motion has a large effect on stopping action with a camera. It's easier to stop the action if the subject is moving toward or away from you. You need higher shutter speeds to stop the motion of subjects crossing your field of vision than you need for other directions of motion.

Another way to help stop the action is to pan your camera with the moving subject. Move your camera smoothly to keep the subject centered

JOHN MENIHAN

Snapping the shutter when the player reached the peak of his jump helped to stop the rapid action of this basketball game.
KODACOLOR 400 Film—1/60 sec f/2 ↓ 2.8

41

in your viewfinder as you take the picture. Your subject will be sharp and the background blurred. This enhances the feeling of motion. Panning works best with a subject moving at a steady speed, such as an ice skater.

Subject distance is also an important factor in stopping action. The farther away you are from your subject, the easier it is to stop the action.

Pan your camera smoothly with a moving subject as you press the shutter release. The blurred background adds a feeling of motion to a still picture. KODACOLOR 400 Film—1/30 sec f/4

KODACOLOR 400 Film allowed the photographer to use a fast shutter speed to stop the action. 1/250 sec f/1.8

Existing light is the best way to photograph stage shows. Flash would interfere with the show and might not be allowed. Usually, flash couldn't carry far enough to light the subjects. KODACOLOR 400 Film—1/125 sec f/2

Stage Shows

Musicals and plays provide beautiful settings for existing-light pictures. Stage productions are easy to photograph because you can use one basic camera setting for most of the show. For example, the camera setting for a typical professional stage show is 1/60 second at $f/4$ with KODAK EKTACHROME 160 Film (Tungsten). Tungsten film will produce the most pleasing color rendition with stage lighting. Focus on a point in the center of the stage about 10 feet behind the footlights to take pictures. You should have enough depth of field for most stages so that refocusing usually isn't necessary.

If there's a lot of action on the stage, you can time your picture-taking to catch brief instants when the actors are relatively motionless. For example, most dance sequences include moments when the dancers pause as they finish a spin or change direction. Slight subject blur, caused by moving arms or legs, for example, can add a feeling of movement to the picture so that it does not look static.

When you use the basic exposure setting given in the table on page 55, your pictures will become lighter or darker as the stage lighting changes, reflecting the mood of the different scenes. When spotlights emphasize one stage area with the rest of the stage dark, your pictures will capture the same effect. When all of the stage is dimly lighted, open your lens 1 stop from the basic exposure. If the lighting is *very* dim, open the lens 2 stops from the basic exposure.

Don't worry if the lower part of your picture includes the heads of a few members of the audience. They will give the picture dimension and help frame the stage. For an unobstructed vantage point, try to get seats in the front row of the balcony. You may want to use a telephoto lens to get close-ups of the actors.

Remember that the people around you want to enjoy the performance, too. Be unobtrusive about your picture-taking so that you don't spoil your neighbors' enjoyment. Some professional theatres prohibit picture-taking during the performance because they feel it detracts from the show.

One of the best times to photograph a stage presentation is during the dress rehearsal. You'll be able to get close to the cast and choose the best viewpoints for your pictures without disturbing an audience.

You'll find possibilities for existing-light pictures at boat shows, auto shows, RV shows, and many others. Move in close if you find interesting detail. Left KODACOLOR 400 Film—1/30 sec f/2.8. Right KODACOLOR 400 Film—1/30 sec f/2.8

Hobby and Trade Shows

When you attend an auto, boat, or flower show, or some other interesting exhibit, you can get colorful and interesting pictures of the displays. The lighting for these shows is provided mainly by overhead lights, which may be tungsten, fluorescent, or mercury vapor. Individual displays often have their own lighting, which may be different from the general overhead lighting. Select color film for the light source that will be predominant in most of your pictures. Use an exposure meter to determine the exposure.

SOME IMPORTANT POINTS TO REMEMBER

- Take a flashlight along so that you can see to make your camera settings under dim lighting conditions.
- Outdoors in cold weather, put your camera under your coat between exposures to keep the shutter working properly.
- A good time to take outdoor night pictures is at twilight, before the sky becomes completely dark.
- For pictures of aerial fireworks displays, put your camera onto a firm support and hold the shutter open for several bursts.
- To help stop the action in sports photography, use a high-speed film and the highest shutter speed that the lighting conditions permit. Then snap the picture at the peak of the action. Panning with the subject also helps stop subject motion in pictures.

The special world of existing light offers many spectacular photo opportunities. The exposure on KODACHROME 25 Film would be 1/30 sec f/5.6

Unusual but true, this picture was taken with only light from the night sky for illumination.

4

DETERMINING EXPOSURE FOR EXISTING-LIGHT PICTURES

Existing light varies considerably in intensity. Since your eyes adapt easily to changes in illumination, they may be deceived by the actual light level in a certain situation. To get correct exposure, use an automatic camera, an exposure meter, or the exposure tables on pages 54-56.

Usually the objective in existing-light photography is to reproduce the scene so that it appears as realistic as possible. Incorrect exposure can drastically alter the way the scene appears in your picture.

Because of the low level of most existing light, underexposure is more common than overexposure. However, you can sometimes overexpose very dimly lighted scenes without realizing it. You'll usually want pictures of scenes such as those found in dark restaurants or outdoors at night to look dark *when the original scene looked dark to you.* But when you use color-slide film and expose these

scenes normally according to an exposure meter, you may give too much exposure. The meter indicates exposures that will make the scenes look average in brightness. As a result, the slides look lighter than the original scenes. The slides may be quite acceptable, but they're not accurate reproductions of the scenes. An example of this effect is a time exposure of a scene lighted by moonlight that appears to have been taken in the daytime. You'll get this effect most often when you photograph dimly lighted scenes that have no lights in them. Lights serve as points of reference as to how light or dark the scene actually appeared.

To make natural-looking color slides of dark scenes, try ½ to 1 stop *less* exposure than the meter indicates. This exposure effect does not apply to negative films because the lightness or darkness of a print is controlled primarily during the printing process.

USING AN EXPOSURE METER IN EXISTING LIGHT

Because the lighting conditions in existing-light scenes vary so widely, an exposure meter or an automatic camera is a big help in determining exposure. However, if you use your meter in a purely mechanical fashion, you may not get consistently good results. Study the instruction book for your meter to learn how to use the meter accurately and to familiarize yourself with the flexibility and limitations of the type of meter you have. This knowledge will help you use your meter effectively under unusual exposure conditions.

In general, there are two kinds of exposure meter. One kind determines exposure by measuring light reflected from the subject. The other measures incident light (the light falling on the subject). Some meters have special attachments that let you measure light by either method. The exposure meters built into cameras are reflected-light meters. Some reflected-light meters measure the light from a large area of the scene, while others measure the light from only part of the scene. The built-in exposure meters in some cameras measure the reflected light coming through the camera lens itself.

In existing-light picture-taking, the way you determine exposure depends on the meter you have and on the illumination.

BOB CLEMENS

Although this scene looks properly exposed, it's actually overexposed—lighter than the scene appeared. EKTACHROME 200 Film (Daylight)—½ sec f/5.6

BOB CLEMENS

This looks more like the original scene. To capture the natural appearance and mood of dim lighting conditions, try ½ to 1 stop less exposure than your meter indicates. EKTACHROME 200 Film (Daylight)—½ sec f/5.6 ↓ 8

49

KODAK EKTACHROME 160 Film (Tungsten)

For Color Slides
135 MAGAZINES

FILM SPEED
ASA 160
With Tungsten
Light 3200 K

This high-speed color-slide film is balanced for 3200 K tungsten lamps. It has improved color rendition, resulting in higher-quality slides. The high speed makes it ideal for taking pictures under existing tungsten light in a variety of situations. By obtaining special processing, you can expose this film at

EXPOSURE

Type of Light	Film Speed	Filter
TUNGSTEN 3200 K	**ASA 160**	**None**
PHOTOLAMPS 3400 K	ASA 125	No. 81A
DAYLIGHT	ASA 100	No. 85B

Note: Exposures longer than 1/8 second may require filtration and exposure compensation.

JOHN MENIHAN

A skylighted room provides even illumination—an easy scene to read with an exposure meter. KODACOLOR 400 Film—1/125 sec f/3.5

NEIL MONTANUS

Making a meter reading from the camera position would result in overexposure because the dark surroundings would mislead the meter. If possible, make a close-up reading of the lighted area. EKTACHROME 160 Film (Tungsten)—1 sec f/5.6

Even Illumination

For scenes with even illumination, it's easy to determine exposure with a meter. Just make a reading of the scene as you normally would for the kind of meter you have. If you're using a reflected-light meter, be careful not to include the light source in your meter reading.

With an incident-light meter, you must adjust the exposure indicated by the meter when the reflectance of the subject is considerably higher or lower than average. If your subject is very light, use ½ stop less exposure than your meter indicates; if the subject is very dark, use ½ to 1 stop more exposure. This exposure adjustment compensates for the lightness or darkness of the subject itself, not for the light illuminating the subject.

Uneven Illumination

Scenes with uneven illumination are quite common in existing-light photography. Uneven lighting often makes your pictures more dramatic, but you will need to exercise more care in making exposure-meter readings under these conditions. Many existing-light scenes—downtown streets and outdoor holiday lighting at night, for example—include large dark areas and smaller lighted areas. In pictures of these scenes, it's usually desirable to have detail in the lighted areas, while the dark or black areas show little or no detail. Expose for the bright areas and let the dark areas go black. You'll find uneven lighting indoors as well. For example, home lighting and the spotlights used to illuminate performers in shows or night-club acts provide uneven lighting conditions. The lighting indoors in daylight is uneven, too, when windows are included in the scene. Since the windows are brighter than the subject in this situation, expose for the darker subject to show detail.

JOHN MENIHAN

Including a window when metering an interior scene can result in underexposure. Move in close to your subject to get a correct exposure reading. EKTACHROME 200 Film (Daylight)—1/125 sec f/5.6

A reflected-light meter used at the camera position usually sees a large area of the scene but doesn't know what parts of the scene are most important to your picture. A reflected-light meter is strongly influenced by large dark or light areas. As a result it indicates the wrong exposure when small, important areas are much lighter or darker than the large, unimportant areas. In these situations, move in to take close-up readings of the important areas.

If different exposures are indicated for different areas of equal importance in the same scene, use the exposure halfway between the correct exposures for the lightest important area and the darkest important area. For example, if 1/30 second at f/5.6 is correct for the lightest *important* part of your picture and 1/30 second at f/2 is correct for the darkest *important* part, then 1/30 second between f/2.8 and f/4 is the best exposure for the picture. Similarly, if you use an incident-light meter to determine exposure for a scene which includes areas of different *illumination* of equal importance, make meter readings in the lightest and darkest important areas of

BOB CLEMENS

Your exposure meter can also be misled by a lighted lamp in the scene. Again, make a close-up reading of your principal subjects, excluding the lamp. EKTACHROME 160 Film (Tungsten)—¼ sec f/8

illumination in the scene. Then use the exposure that's halfway between the exposures indicated by your meter.

Bright lights in the scene can mislead your reflected-light exposure meter, making the reading too high and causing underexposure. To get the correct exposure, either *shield the meter* with your hand to block out the light source or make a *close-up reading* of your subject. When a light source, say a neon sign, is the subject, make a close-up reading of the light source with a reflected-light meter and expose according to the meter.

Since an incident-light exposure meter measures the light falling on the scene, it won't be misled by a bright window or other lights in the scene. But usually you must move close to your subject so that you can place the meter in the same light that is lighting the subject.

Spot Meters

For scenes with uneven illumination or uneven subject brightness that would require close-up meter readings with an ordinary reflected-light meter, you can use a spot meter from the camera position to determine exposure.

A spot meter is a reflected-light exposure meter that makes a reading of one small area in the scene at a time. Some cameras have built-in meters that can make spot readings. A spot meter is especially helpful when you can't make a close-up meter reading—photographing spotlighted performers at a circus, for example.

Spot meters are also useful when you use a telephoto lens, which includes only a small area of the overall scene that would be read by an ordinary reflected-light meter. However, you usually must make more than one reading of different parts of the subject to determine the best exposure,

even with uniformly lighted scenes. This is necessary because small areas of the subject usually differ in brightness. As a result, using a spot meter is more time-consuming and requires more experience than a conventional exposure meter.

Exposure-Meter Sensitivity

In existing-light photography, you need a sensitive exposure meter that can accurately measure low levels of illumination. Many exposure meters and automatic cameras have battery-powered cells that work well under dim lighting conditions. However, some older meters and automatic cameras are not sensitive enough to measure accurately the exposures required for dimly lighted existing-light scenes.

If your reflected-light exposure meter is not sensitive enough to indicate a reading for a dimly lighted scene, or if the reading is too low on the meter scale to be reliable, you can make a substitute meter reading from a white handkerchief or a piece of white paper. Divide the film speed by 5 and set this lower number on the dial of your exposure meter to determine the exposure. Then place the handkerchief or paper in the same light that is illuminating your subject and make the meter reading.

If your exposure meter is just not sensitive enough to respond to the dim lighting, you can set your manually adjustable camera according to the exposure tables in this book or the recommendations given on some film instruction sheets.

USING EXPOSURE TABLES

For certain scenes that can mislead your meter or for situations in which it's impractical to make a close-up reading, an exposure table may be more reliable than an exposure meter.

The suggested exposures given in the tables on pages 54-56 are based on pictures taken by experienced photographers. The exposures are typical for the subjects listed. However, because specific conditions vary, you should use these recommendations as *guides* only.

BRACKETING EXPOSURES

If you are doubtful about the correct exposure for an especially important photograph, bracket your exposure. Take one picture at the exposure indicated by your meter or suggested in an exposure table, and then take two more pictures—one at 1 stop less and one at 1 stop more than the estimated exposure. If you want even more insurance, make two *more* pictures—one at 2 stops under and another at 2 stops over the estimated exposure.

Your ability to determine exposure will improve as you gain experience in taking existing-light pictures. You'll get a higher percentage of properly exposed pictures if you record your exposure data for various subjects—especially unusual ones—and then refer to these exposures when you encounter similar situations. In existing-light photography it's often a good idea to experiment. Judge the exposure as accurately as you can, and then take the picture. You'll usually be pleased with the results.

This exposure series shows the result of bracketing exposure. Exposure settings shown are for EKTACHROME 400 Film (Daylight).

MARTY TAYLOR

⅛ sec f/2—
2 stops increase in exposure

1/15 sec f/2—
1 stop increase in exposure

1/30 sec f/2—
estimated exposure

1/30 sec f/2.8—
1 stop decrease in exposure

1/30 sec f/4—
2 stops decrease in exposure

SUGGESTED EXPOSURES FOR *KODAK* FILMS

Picture Subject	KODACHROME 64 (Daylight), ASA 64* / EKTACHROME 64 (Daylight), ASA 64 / KODACOLOR II, ASA 100	EKTACHROME 200 (Daylight), ASA 200 / EKTACHROME 160 (Tungsten), ASA 160 normal processing / VERICHROME Pan, ASA 125 / PLUS-X Pan, ASA 125	EKTACHROME 400 (Daylight), ASA 400—normal processing / EKTACHROME 200 (Daylight), ASA 400— EKTACHROME 160 (Tungsten), ASA 320— ESP-1 Processing for 2 times normal film speed / KODACOLOR 400, ASA 400 / TRI-X Pan, ASA 400	EKTACHROME 400 (Daylight), ASA 800— ESP-1 Processing for 2 times normal film speed	ROYAL-X Pan, ASA 1250 / 2475 Recording (ESTAR-AH Base), speed 1000
AT HOME					
Home interiors at night—Areas with average light / Areas with bright light	$1/4$ sec f/2.8 / $1/15$ sec f/2	$1/15$ sec f/2 / $1/30$ sec f/2	$1/30$ sec f/2 / $1/30$ sec f/2.8	$1/30$ sec f/2.8 / $1/30$ sec f/4	$1/30$ sec f/4 / $1/60$ sec f/4
Candlelighted close-ups	$1/4$ sec f/2	$1/8$ sec f/2	$1/15$ sec f/2	$1/30$ sec f/2	$1/30$ sec f/2.8
OUTDOORS AT NIGHT					
Indoor and outdoor holiday lighting at night, Christmas trees	1 sec f/4	1 sec f/5.6	$1/15$ sec f/2	$1/30$ sec f/2	$1/30$ sec f/2.8
Brightly lighted downtown street scenes (Wet streets add interesting reflections.)	$1/30$ sec f/2	$1/30$ sec f/2.8	$1/60$ sec f/2.8	$1/60$ sec f/4	$1/125$ sec f/4
Brightly lighted nightclub or theatre districts—Las Vegas or Times Square	$1/30$ sec f/2.8	$1/30$ sec f/4	$1/60$ sec f/4	$1/125$ sec f/4	$1/125$ sec f/5.6
Neon signs and other lighted signs	$1/30$ sec f/4	$1/60$ sec f/4	$1/125$ sec f/4	$1/125$ sec f/5.6	$1/125$ sec f/8
Store windows	$1/30$ sec f/2.8	$1/30$ sec f/4	$1/60$ sec f/4	$1/60$ sec f/5.6	$1/60$ sec f/8
Subjects lighted by streetlights	$1/4$ sec f/2	$1/8$ sec f/2	$1/15$ sec f/2	$1/30$ sec f/2	$1/30$ sec f/2.8
Floodlighted buildings, fountains, monuments	1 sec f/4	$1/2$ sec f/4	$1/15$ sec f/2	$1/30$ sec f/2	$1/30$ sec f/2.8
Skyline—distant view of lighted buildings at night	4 sec f/2.8	1 sec f/2	1 sec f/2.8	1 sec f/4	1 sec f/5.6
Skyline—10 minutes after sunset	$1/30$ sec f/4	$1/60$ sec f/4	$1/60$ sec f/5.6	$1/125$ sec f/5.6	$1/125$ sec f/8

OUTDOORS AT NIGHT	Fairs, amusement parks	1/15 sec f/2	1/30 sec f/2	1/30 sec f/2.8	1/60 sec f/2.8	1/60 sec f/4
	Amusement park rides—light patterns	4 sec f/16	2 sec f/16	1 sec f/16	1 sec f/22	—
	Fireworks—displays on the ground	1/30 sec f/2.8	1/30 sec f/4	1/60 sec f/4	1/60 sec f/5.6	1/60 sec f/8
	Fireworks—aerial displays (Keep shutter open on Bulb or Time for several bursts.)	f/8	f/11	f/16	f/22	f/32
	Lightning (Keep shutter open on Bulb or Time for one or two streaks of lightning.)	f/5.6	f/8	f/11	f/16	f/22
	Burning buildings, campfires, bonfires	1/30 sec f/2.8	1/30 sec f/4	1/60 sec f/4	1/60 sec f/5.6	1/125 sec f/5.6
	Subjects by campfires, bonfires	1/8 sec f/2	1/15 sec f/2	1/30 sec f/2	1/30 sec f/2.8	1/30 sec f/4
	Night football, baseball, racetracks†	1/30 sec f/2.8	1/60 sec f/2.8	1/125 sec f/2.8	1/250 sec f/2.8	1/250 sec f/4
	Niagara Falls—White lights	15 sec f/5.6	8 sec f/5.6	4 sec f/5.6	4 sec f/8	4 sec f/11
	Light-colored lights	30 sec f/5.6	15 sec f/5.6	8 sec f/5.6	4 sec f/5.6	4 sec f/8
	Dark-colored lights	30 sec f/4	30 sec f/5.6	15 sec f/5.6	8 sec f/5.6	4 sec f/5.6
	Moonlighted—Landscapes	30 sec f/2	15 sec f/2	8 sec f/2	4 sec f/2	4 sec f/2.8
	Snow scenes	15 sec f/2	8 sec f/2	4 sec f/2.8	4 sec f/2.8	4 sec f/4
INDOORS IN PUBLIC PLACES	Basketball, hockey, bowling	1/30 sec f/2	1/60 sec f/2	1/125 sec f/2	1/125 sec f/2.8	1/250 sec f/2.8
	Boxing, wrestling	1/60 sec f/2	1/125 sec f/2	1/250 sec f/2	1/250 sec f/2.8	1/250 sec f/4
	Stage shows—Average	1/30 sec f/2	1/30 sec f/2.8	1/60 sec f/2.8	1/125 sec f/2.8	1/125 sec f/4
	Bright	1/60 sec f/2.8	1/60 sec f/4	1/125 sec f/4	1/125 sec f/2.8	1/250 sec f/5.6
	Circuses—Floodlighted acts	1/30 sec f/2	1/30 sec f/2.8	1/60 sec f/2.8	1/125 sec f/2.8	1/250 sec f/2.8
	Spotlighted acts (carbon-arc)	1/60 sec f/2.8	1/125 sec f/2.8	1/250 sec f/2.8	1/250 sec f/4	1/250 sec f/5.6
	Ice shows—Floodlighted acts	1/30 sec f/2.8	1/60 sec f/2.8	1/125 sec f/2.8	1/250 sec f/2.8	1/250 sec f/4
	Spotlighted acts (carbon-arc)	1/60 sec f/2.8	1/125 sec f/2.8	1/250 sec f/2.8	1/250 sec f/4	1/250 sec f/5.6
	Interiors with bright fluorescent light	1/30 sec f/2.8	1/30 sec f/4	1/60 sec f/4	1/60 sec f/5.6	1/125 sec f/5.6
	School—stage and auditorium	—	1/15 sec f/2	1/30 sec f/2	1/30 sec f/2.8	1/30 sec f/4

SUGGESTED EXPOSURES FOR KODAK FILMS (Continued)

Picture Subject	KODACHROME 64 (Daylight), ASA 64* EKTACHROME 64 (Daylight), ASA 64 KODACOLOR II, ASA 100	EKTACHROME 200 (Daylight), ASA 200 EKTACHROME 160 (Tungsten), ASA 160 normal processing VERICHROME Pan, ASA 125 PLUS-X Pan, ASA 125	EKTACHROME 400 (Daylight), ASA 400—normal processing EKTACHROME 200 (Daylight), ASA 400—EKTACHROME 160 (Tungsten), ASA 320—ESP-1 Processing for 2 times normal film speed KODACOLOR 400, ASA 400 TRI-X Pan, ASA 400	EKTACHROME 400 (Daylight), ASA 800—ESP-1 Processing for 2 times normal film speed	ROYAL-X Pan, ASA 1250 2475 Recording (ESTAR-AH Base), speed 1000
INDOORS IN PUBLIC PLACES Swimming pool—tungsten light indoors (above water)	1/15 sec f/2	1/30 sec f/2	1/60 sec f/2	1/60 sec f/2.8	1/60 sec f/4
Hospital nurseries	1/30 sec f/2	1/30 sec f/2.8	1/60 sec f/2.8	1/60 sec f/4	1/125 sec f/4
Church interiors—tungsten light	1 sec f/5.6	1/15 sec f/2	1/30 sec f/2	1/30 sec f/2.8	1/30 sec f/4
Stained-glass windows, daytime—photographed from inside	Use 3 stops more exposure than for the outdoor lighting conditions.				
Glassware in windows, daytime—photographed from inside	Use 1 stop more exposure than for the outdoor lighting conditions.				

*You can take pictures on KODACHROME 25 Film (Daylight) by using approximately 1 stop more exposure than recommended for KODACHROME 64 Film (Daylight).

†When the lighting at these events is provided by mercury-vapor lamps, you'll get better results by using Daylight film. However, your pictures will still appear greenish.

Use a tripod or other firm support for shutter speeds slower than 1/30 second.

With KODACOLOR Films you can take pictures of all the scenes listed in the tables and get acceptable color quality.

For color pictures of these scenes, use Tungsten film for the most natural rendition. You can also use Daylight color film, but your pictures will look yellow-red.

For color pictures of these scenes, use Daylight film. You can also use Tungsten film with a No. 85B filter over your camera lens. When you use this filter, give 1 stop more exposure than that recommended for daylight film in the table.

For color pictures of these scenes, you can use either Daylight or Tungsten film. Daylight film will produce colors with a warmer, more yellowish look. Tungsten film produces colors with a colder, more bluish appearance.

Candlelight—EKTACHROME 160 Film (Tungsten)—1 sec f/4 ↓ 5.6

57

EKTACHROME 400 Film (Daylight)—1/30 sec f/2.8 ↓ 4

SOME IMPORTANT POINTS TO REMEMBER

- With a reflected-light meter, make a close-up reading of the principal subject when
  1. bright lights or a window included in the scene may mislead your meter.
  2. the surroundings are much darker or lighter than the subject.
  3. a light source, such as a neon sign, is the subject.
- If you are using an incident-light meter, make an exposure compensation when the subject is either very light or very dark. For a very light subject, use ½ stop less exposure than your meter indicates; for a very dark subject, use ½ to 1 stop more exposure than the meter indicates.
- For scenes with uneven lighting, make separate meter readings of important areas in the scene, and use the exposure halfway between the exposure that is correct for the lightest important area and the exposure that is correct for the darkest important area.
- If a scene is difficult to meter or if you don't have an exposure meter or an automatic camera, try the exposure given in the tables on pages 54-56.

5
CAMERA-HANDLING TECHNIQUES

Good stance
for holding the
camera steady

TECHNIQUES FOR SHARP PICTURES

The slowest recommended exposure time for picture-taking with a hand-held camera and a normal focal-length lens is 1/30 second (1/25 second with older cameras), which you will have to use for adequate exposure in many existing-light situations. Even in brighter situations you may want to leave the shutter speed at 1/30 second and use a small lens opening to increase depth of field. (See page 60.)

Here are some techniques that will help you minimize or eliminate camera motion and obtain sharp pictures.

- Brace yourself with your elbows against your body, and stand with your feet slightly apart for a good solid stance.
- If possible, brace your body against a solid object such as a lamppost or a wall.
- Hold your camera very steady and press the shutter release slowly and gently.
- Use a higher shutter speed, such as 1/125 second, when lighting conditions permit or when you don't need to use a small lens opening for great depth of field.
- For shutter speeds slower than 1/30 second, put your camera onto a tripod, table, or ledge; fasten it with a camera clamp; or brace it against a wall.
- Use a cable release or a self-timer to trip the camera shutter.
- Practice holding your unloaded camera as steady as possible and tripping the shutter.

Mirror test for camera steadiness

TIME EXPOSURES

Although it's possible to take hand-held pictures of most subjects, you can take better pictures of certain subjects by making time exposures with your camera on a firm support. For example, time exposures of street scenes will record light patterns made by moving cars. When you make time exposures, you can use smaller lens openings to increase depth of field. Time exposures also let you take existing-light pictures with a camera that has a slow lens or with a slower-speed film.

When you use long exposure times, the characteristics of your film can change. The effects of time exposures are discussed on page 70.

Try a simple mirror test to check on the steadiness of your camera-holding and shutter-tripping techniques. Tape a small mirror to the front of your camera. In a darkened room, direct the light from a flashlight or projector toward the mirror. Hold your camera as you would for taking pictures and direct the light reflection so that you can see it on a wall several feet away. As you trip the camera shutter, watch the spot of light. If the spot jumps, you are moving the camera as you release the shutter. With a little practice, you'll be able to hold the camera steady.

With a telephoto lens, you should use a higher shutter speed for hand-held pictures, or put your camera onto a tripod to eliminate camera motion. A telephoto lens magnifies the effect of camera movement to the same degree that it magnifies the image of the subject. When you use a 135 mm telephoto lens, the image is almost 3 times as large as that produced by a 50 mm lens at the same distance from the subject. Therefore, the minimum shutter speed for handholding a 35 mm camera with a 135 mm lens would be 3 times as fast as for a 50 mm lens, or about 1/125 second.

DEPTH OF FIELD

Depth of field is the distance range between the nearest and farthest points in the scene that appear to be in sharp focus in your picture. Since depth of field is shallow with the large lens openings required for many existing-light pictures, it's important to focus your camera accurately.

Most adjustable cameras have depth-of-field scales which indicate the range of sharp focus. With some single-lens reflex cameras you can also see what the depth of field will be when you look through the viewfinder. (Check your camera instruction manual.) If your camera doesn't show depth of field, your camera manual may include depth-of-field tables. The *KODAK Master Photoguide* (AR-21), sold by photo dealers, contains a handy Depth-of-Field Computer.

If you want the greatest possible depth of field with a stationary subject, you may want to put your camera onto a steady support and use a longer exposure time and a smaller lens opening.

Streaks of light from moving traffic create interesting patterns and a look of action against the Los Angeles skyline just after sunset. The camera was on a tripod for an exposure of 30 sec at *f*/22.

Since depth of field is shallow at large lens openings, focusing your camera on the subject throws the background out of focus and helps direct attention to the subject. KODACOLOR 400 Film—1/125 sec *f*/2.8

A moving amusement park ride made this dazzling pattern during an exposure of 1/30 sec at f/2.8 on EKTACHROME 160 Film (Tungsten).

SOME IMPORTANT POINTS TO REMEMBER

- Hold your camera steady and carefully *press* the shutter release to take the picture.
- Use a camera support for shutter speeds slower than 1/30 second.
- For handheld picture-taking with a telephoto lens on your camera, use a higher shutter speed than you would with a normal-focal-length lens.
- With your camera on a firm support, use slow shutter speeds or short time exposures when your lens or the speed of your film is not fast enough for handheld shots, when you want to use a small lens opening for more depth of field, or when you want blurred motion in your pictures.
- Focus accurately because depth of field is very shallow at the large lens openings you'll use. You can gain more depth of field by using a smaller lens opening and a slower shutter speed when the picture-taking situation permits.

MARTY TAYLOR

CAROLINE GRIMES

High-speed EKTACHROME Films are good choices for taking color slides by existing light—they have excellent color quality and very fine grain. Top EKTACHROME 200 Film (Daylight)—1/30 sec f/2.8. Bottom EKTACHROME 160 Film (Tungsten)— 1/30 sec f/1.4

6
KODAK FILMS FOR EXISTING-LIGHT PHOTOGRAPHY

After you have decided what kind of pictures you want—color slides or color or black-and-white prints—one of the most important factors to consider in selecting a film for existing-light picture-taking is film speed. As we've mentioned before, since low light levels are very common in existing-light photography, it's best to use a high-speed film. You can use a film with a slower speed when you take pictures where there is a high light level, such as near windows or a skylight, or when you put your camera onto a tripod and use long exposure times.

COLOR FILM

Film for Color Slides

When you want color slides, one of the high-speed KODAK EKTACHROME Films would be a good choice. There are two Daylight films—EKTACHROME 400 Film and EKTACHROME 200 Film —with ASA ratings of 400 and 200 respectively. The Tungsten film, EKTACHROME 160, has ASA speed 160. With special processing by Kodak or other labs (or even yourself), you can increase the speed of these films 2 times. See pages 71 and 72 for information about increasing film speed.

For those situations that don't require a high-speed film, you can use KODAK EKTACHROME 64 Film (Daylight) and KODACHROME 64 Film (Daylight) for color slides. These films have medium speed and are designed for daylight (or blue flash).

KODACHROME 25 Film (Daylight) is not fast enough for most existing-light photography, except for situations in which you can put your camera onto a tripod and use long exposure times.

Film for Color Prints

When you want color prints, try KODACOLOR 400 Film. This high-speed film is recommended for use with daylight (or blue flash) without filters. You can also get good color prints when you use KODACOLOR 400 Film under tungsten or fluorescent illumination without filters. For critical color balance with illumination other than daylight you may want to use a filter. See pages 67 and 69 for filter recommendations. You can also use KODACOLOR II Film, which has a moderate speed of ASA 100, color-balanced for daylight and blue flash. Again, you can use KODACOLOR II Film with illumination other than sunlight. Some color correction can be

DON MAGGIO

With existing daylight indoors, you can usually take handheld pictures on medium-speed film. EKTACHROME 64 Film (Daylight)—1/30 sec f/5.6 ↓ 8

KODACOLOR 400 Film gives you color prints. It has very high speed, wide exposure latitude, extremely fine grain, and the ability to adapt to a wide range of illumination color quality. The latitude of KODACOLOR 400 helps minimize exposure error and the light-color adaptability helps get good color pictures under a variety of lighting conditions. KODACOLOR 400 Film with light from kerosene lamp, 1/15 sec f/2.8

LOWELL MILLER

Taken with fluorescent light.
KODACOLOR 400 Film—
1/30 sec f/4

Taken with a combination of daylight
and tungsten light. KODACOLOR
400 Film—1/60 sec f/2

made when the negatives are printed. If you need accurate color reproduction, consider using a color correction filter. See pages 67 and 69.

Prints from Slides and Slides from Negatives

You can have additional color slides or color prints and enlargements made from your color slides. From your color negatives, you can order color prints and enlargements, color slides, or black-and-white prints. All of these services, except for color slides from 110-size color negatives and black-and-white processing, are available from Kodak. Other photofinishers may offer all the services. See your photo dealer.

CHOOSING COLOR FILM FOR THE TYPE OF ILLUMINATION

For the most faithful color reproduction in your pictures, use a film that is recommended for light similar to the lighting on your subject. In existing-light photography, however, color reproduction is not as critical as in other kinds of picture-taking, because the natural appearance of the lighting compensates to a large extent for color rendition that may be less than ideal. In addition, when you project slides in a darkened room, no color references will be visible. When colored lights, such as neon signs or holiday lighting, are included in the picture, variation in color reproduction is acceptable.

MARTY TAYLOR

The picture on top, taken on EKTACHROME 160 Film (Tungsten), shows the natural appearance of the tungsten lighting on the totem. EKTACHROME 200 Film (Daylight) was used for the warmer shot on the bottom. Many people would find both pictures acceptable. 1/60 sec at f/2 for both—normal processing

Daylight Illumination

Daylight color film is designed for use with daylight, blue flash, or electronic flash. You can also use Daylight film with carbon-arc spotlights, which have a color quality similar to that of daylight. If you expose Tungsten film with daylight illumination, use a No. 85B filter to obtain good color rendition. Without the filter, your pictures will be unacceptably bluish.

Tungsten Illumination

Tungsten film is recommended for use with 3200 K photolamps, but it's excellent for existing tungsten light, such as the light from lamps in your home. Even though most tungsten lights are slightly warmer in color than 3200 K photolamps, we accept warm-looking pictures because most indoor scenes lighted by tungsten illumination have a naturally warm appearance. If you use Daylight film for tungsten light, your pictures will probably be acceptable, but they'll have a yellow-red cast.

Fluorescent Illumination

Fluorescent illumination can cause odd color rendition in your pictures, since most fluorescent lamps are deficient in red. Daylight color film is best for fluorescent lighting, although your pictures will probably still look greenish. Tungsten film usually produces pictures that are much too blue.

You can improve the color quality of pictures taken under fluorescent illumination by bouncing light from electronic flash off a white ceiling or by using filters over your camera lens. However, it's usually not practical to use filters in existing light because they absorb too much light and reduce the effective speed of the film. Selecting filters for fluorescent illumination is sometimes difficult because there are many kinds of fluorescent lamps

KODAK COLOR FILMS IN ROLLS SUGGESTED FOR EXISTING-LIGHT PICTURES

KODAK Color Film	ASA Speed	Type of Existing Light	Use for	Sizes Available	Processed by	Process
EKTACHROME 400 (Daylight)	400 800*	daylight, fluorescent, or outdoors at night	color slides	135-20, 135-36, 120	Kodak, other labs, or users	E-6
EKTACHROME 200 (Daylight)	200 400*	daylight, fluorescent, or outdoors at night	color slides	135-20, 135-36, 126-20**	Kodak, other labs, or users	E-6
EKTACHROME 160 (Tungsten)	160 320*	tungsten or outdoors at night	color slides	135-20, 135-36**	Kodak, other labs, or users	E-6
	100† 200*†	daylight with No. 85B filter	color slides			
EKTACHROME 64 (Daylight)	64	daylight, fluorescent, or outdoors at night	color slides	135-20, 135-36, 126-20, 110-20, 127**	Kodak, other labs, or users	E-6
KODACHROME 64 (Daylight)	64	daylight, fluorescent, or outdoors at night	color slides	135-20, 135-36, 126-20, 110-20	Kodak or other labs	commercial laboratory (K-14)
KODACOLOR 400	400	daylight, tungsten, fluorescent, or outdoors at night‡	color prints	135-24, 135-36, 110-12, 110-20, 120	Kodak, other labs, or users	C-41
KODACOLOR II	100	daylight, tungsten, fluorescent, or outdoors at night‡	color prints	135-24, 135-36, 126-12, 126-20, 110-12, 110-20, 828, 127, 620, 120, 616, 116	Kodak, other labs, or users	C-41

*You can expose high-speed KODAK EKTACHROME Films, 120 or 135 size, at the speeds shown when you use the KODAK Special Processing Envelope, ESP-1, sold by photo dealers. See page 71.

**A professional version of this film is available in the 120 size.

‡See page 64 for explanation. For critical color rendition under tungsten light, use a No. 80A filter and increase exposure 2 stops.

†With most cameras that have built-in exposure meters which make the light reading through the No. 85B filter over the lens, you can set the film-speed dial on your camera for the speed of the Tungsten film without a filter: either 160 or 320, depending on whether you use the ESP-1 Envelope. However, camera instructions vary, so check your camera manual for how to set this type of exposure meter.

If you use Tungsten film without a filter for pictures in fluorescent light, they'll be bluish. EKTACHROME 160 Film (Tungsten), no filter—1/30 sec f/5.6

You can use Daylight film without a filter under fluorescent light. Color rendition will be slightly off, depending on the kind of fluorescent lamps. EKTACHROME 200 Film (Daylight), no filter—1/30 sec f/5.6

For best color rendition under fluorescent illumination, use a filter over your lens, and Daylight film in your camera. EKTACHROME 200 Film (Daylight) with CC30M filter—1/30 sec f/4.5. Exposure was increased 2/3 stop to compensate for the filter.

and each kind produces light of a slightly different color. But if optimum color rendition is important and the kind of lamp is known, you can improve the color in your pictures by using the KODAK Color Compensating Filters (available from photo dealers) recommended in the table on the next page. If you can't find out the kind of fluorescent lamps, you can use a compromise filter. For Daylight film, use a CC30M filter and a 2/3 stop increase in exposure. With Tungsten film, use a CC50R filter with 1 stop increase in exposure.

Because of the increase in exposure, taking handheld pictures with filters is limited to scenes with highlight levels, such as in schools, offices, and factories. In locations with lower levels of fluorescent light, you'll probably have to put your camera onto a support and use exposure times longer than 1/30 second.

Mercury-Vapor Illumination

There are several different types and brands of mercury-vapor lamps. Most of them are deficient in red light, so they often require heavy filtration for good color balance in pictures. With some of these lamps, no amount of filtration will produce good color rendition.

Since it's improbable that you could find out the kind of lamps being used and the heavy filtration required would necessitate a large increase in exposure, it's impractical to recommend filters for mercury-vapor illumination. Under this lighting, you'll get the best results on Daylight film, but pictures will usually have a blue-green cast.

FILTERS FOR FLUORESCENT LIGHT		
KODAK Color Film		
Fluorescent Lamp	**KODACHROME 64 (Daylight)** **EKTACHROME 64 (Daylight)** **EKTACHROME 200 (Daylight)** **EKTACHROME 400 (Daylight)** **KODACOLOR II*** **KODACOLOR 400***	**EKTACHROME 160 (Tungsten)**
Daylight	40M + 30Y + 1 stop	No. 85B + 30M + 10Y + 1⅔ stops
White	20C + 30M + 1 stop	40M + 40Y + 1 stop
Warm White	40C + 40M + 1⅓ stops	30M + 20Y + 1 stop
Warm White Deluxe	60C + 30M + 1⅔ stops	10Y + ⅓ stop
Cool White	30M + ⅔ stop	50M + 60Y + 1⅓ stop
Cool White Deluxe	30C + 20M + 1 stop	10M + 30Y + ⅔ stop

Note: Increase exposure by amount shown in table.

---

*If you're not concerned with critical color rendition under fluorescent illumination, you'll find that KODACOLOR 400 and KODACOLOR II Films provide acceptable results without additional filters.

Mixed Light Sources

Sometimes you will find more than one kind of illumination in the same scene. If one light source is predominant, use color film intended for that light source. For example, in a scene which includes both daylight and tungsten light, daylight is usually the predominant light source, and Daylight film would give the most pleasing results. If the kinds of illumination in the scene are about equal in intensity and distribution, the choice of color film is a matter of personal taste. If you like warmer-looking pictures, use Daylight film; if you prefer colder-looking pictures, use Tungsten film.

The illumination in this scene is a combination of overhead fluorescent lighting and tungsten light from the desk lamp. Since the fluorescent lights are providing most of the light, Daylight film is the better choice, as shown in the picture on the top—EKTACHROME 200 Film (Daylight)—1/30 sec f/2.8. The shot on the bottom was made on EKTACHROME 160 Film (Tungsten)—1/30 sec f/2.8

LYNNE TAYLOR

69

BOB CLEMENS

A combination of daylight and tungsten light looks best on Daylight film as shown in the top picture. The Tungsten-film version is on the bottom.

Daylight and Tungsten-Light Scenes on the Same Roll of Color-Slide Film

If you want to photograph some scenes with daylight illumination and others with tungsten illumination on the same roll of color-slide film, use KODAK EKTACHROME 160 Film (Tungsten). For the daylight scenes, use a No. 85B filter over your camera lens.

THE EFFECTS OF LONG EXPOSURE TIMES ON COLOR FILMS

Most color films are designed for the typical short exposure times used in general picture-taking. At longer exposure times (approximately 1 second for most films), film speed will begin to decrease and color rendition will shift away from normal. These changes are referred to as the reciprocity characteristics of the film.

You can correct for the reciprocity effect by using filters and increasing the exposure. Since it's not often practical in existing-light photography to use filters, you can increase exposure to compensate for the decrease in film speed. (You can avoid the reciprocity effect simply by using shutter speeds shorter than 1 second when practical.)

Long time exposures are useful for some outdoor scenes at night, when color rendition usually is not critical, and often, neither is exposure. When you want to compensate for the reciprocity effect for Kodak color films, however, increase your estimated exposure. For a 1-second exposure, use a lens opening 1 stop larger; for an exposure of 10 seconds or longer, use a lens opening 1½ stops larger. Specific exposure and filter corrections for reciprocity characteristics of Kodak color films are given in the book *KODAK Films—Color and Black-and-White* (AF-1), available from your photo dealer. The information is also available by writing to Kodak—you'll find the address for Department 841 on page 80.

PROCESSING COLOR FILM

Have your film processed promptly after exposure. Return Kodak color film to your dealer for processing by Kodak or another laboratory, or mail it directly to Kodak in the appropriate mailer (for prepaid processing).

You can process KODACOLOR and KODAK EKTACHROME Films yourself in processing kits sold by photo dealers. All the necessary chemicals and directions for processing the film are included in the kits.

KODAK Special Processing Envelope, ESP-1

In existing-light picture-taking, you'll frequently find that you need all the film speed you can get. By taking advantage of Special Processing for EKTACHROME Films by Kodak, you can increase the film speed of high-speed EKTACHROME Films 2 times which gives EKTACHROME 400 Film (Daylight) an ASA rating of 800, EKTACHROME 200 Film (Daylight), ASA 400, and EKTACHROME 160 Film (Tungsten), ASA 320. If your camera has an f/2 or faster lens, this extra film speed will let you photograph almost all existing-light scenes while handholding your camera set at 1/30 second or higher and the proper lens opening. When you're photographing more brightly lighted scenes, the increased film speed lets you use small lens openings for more depth of

field, or higher shutter speeds to stop action. Special Processing is available for high-speed EKTACHROME Films in the 135 and 120 sizes. *In an emergency, expose* EKTACHROME 64 Film (Daylight) in sizes 135 and 120 at a speed of *ASA 125,* and obtain Special Processing for EKTACHROME Film by Kodak.

To get the special processing, buy a KODAK Special Processing Envelope, ESP-1, from your photo dealer. The cost of the ESP-1 Envelope is in addition to the charge for regular processing by Kodak. After you've exposed the film at the increased film speed, put the roll into the envelope, and take it to your photo dealer for special processing by Kodak or other laboratories; or mail it directly to a U.S. Kodak Processing Laboratory in the appropriate KODAK Mailer (for Prepaid Processing).

Push-Processing KODAK EKTACHROME Film Yourself

You can push-process KODAK EKTACHROME Films yourself with the KODAK EKTACHROME Film Processing Kit, Process E-6. Simply increase the normal developing time in the first developer by the amount given in the table on the next page. For all the other steps, follow the normal processing times in the instructions that come with the chemicals.

The quality of EKTACHROME Films with special processing for higher speeds is quite good. Graininess and contrast are increased somewhat, but the benefits from higher film speeds for existing-light pictures are usually more important than a slight loss of quality.

PUSH-PROCESSING *KODAK EKTACHROME* FILMS IN *KODAK EKTACHROME* FILM CHEMICALS, PROCESS E-6				
ASA Film Speed				Change the time in the first developer by
EKTACHROME 400 (Daylight)	EKTACHROME 200 (Daylight)	EKTACHROME 160 (Tungsten)	EKTACHROME 64 (Daylight)	
1600	800	640	250	+ 5½ minutes
800	400	320	125	+ 2 minutes

MARTY TAYLOR

The increase in film speed provided by ESP-1 Processing enables you to take handheld pictures of very dimly lighted subjects. The exposure for this scene would be 1/30 sec at f/2 on EKTACHROME 400 Film (Daylight)—ASA 800 with ESP-1 Processing.

JOHN MENIHAN

The color quality and sharpness of this picture have captured the glittering action of the Ice Follies. EKTACHROME 200 Film (Daylight)—ASA 400 with ESP-1 Processing, 1/250 sec f/2.5

S. BRADLEY, KINSA

The delicate interplay of tones in this picture help capture the softness and emotion of a mother and infant situation. KODAK PLUS-X Pan Film—ASA 125

B. WHITE, KINSA

The high speed and fine grain of KODAK TRI-X Pan Film make it an excellent film to use for black-and-white existing-light pictures. TRI-X Pan Film—ASA 400

BLACK-AND-WHITE FILM

When you take black-and-white pictures in existing light, you don't have to be concerned with the color of the light source. Also, there are very high-speed black-and-white films for which exposure is less critical than with color-slide films. Many salon exhibitors enjoy working with black-and-white materials because they have complete control over their results during the film-developing and enlarging processes. Certain scenes, such as those which have a minimum of color and those in which you want to capture the starkness of a subject, are sometimes best portrayed in black-and-white pictures.

Types of Black-and-White Films

Modern black-and-white films offer you the versatility of high film speeds with a minimum of graininess. For example, KODAK TRI-X Pan Film has a speed of ASA 400, which is sufficient for most handheld existing-light pictures. Yet it has fine grain and excellent sharpness, which allow you to make big enlargements with good definition.

For bright scenes, you can use a slower, finer-grain film, KODAK VERICHROME Pan Film or KODAK PLUS-X Pan Film, for example. Both films have a speed of ASA 125.

When you want to photograph action in a scene with a very low light

KODAK BLACK-AND-WHITE FILMS IN ROLLS SUGGESTED FOR EXISTING-LIGHT PICTURES

KODAK Film	ASA Speed	Graininess	Sizes
VERICHROME Pan	125	Extremely Fine	126-12, 110-12, 127, 120, 620
PLUS-X Pan	125	Extremely Fine	135-20, 135-36
TRI-X Pan	400	Fine	126-12, 135-20, 135-36, 120
2475 Recording (ESTAR-AH Base)	1000	Coarse	135-36
ROYAL-X Pan	1250	Medium	120

B. BRAINERD, SKPA*

The high speed of TRI-X Pan Film permitted the photographer to use a very fast shutter speed to stop the action. TRI-X Pan Film— ASA 400, 1/500 sec f/2.8

*Courtesy Scholastic/Kodak Photography Awards.

level, you can use an extremely high-speed film such as KODAK Recording Film 2475 (ESTAR-AH Base), speed 1000, or KODAK ROYAL-X Pan Film, ASA 1250. (For most applications with Recording Film 2475, you can use a film speed of 1600.) Because of their extremely high speeds, these films have coarser grain.

The table above will help you select a black-and-white film for your existing-light photography.

Exposure Latitude

Black-and-white films have more camera exposure latitude than color-slide (reversal) films. *You'll obtain the best quality in your pictures when they are properly exposed.* But a film with wide exposure latitude will produce a good picture even though it may be somewhat overexposed or underexposed. Negative films generally have more exposure latitude for overexposure than for underexposure.

Many existing-light scenes have either average or high contrast. Under these conditions, you should determine exposure according to the ASA speed of your film. When you photograph evenly lighted scenes that have lower-than-average contrast (few shadows, for instance), you can get by with less-than-normal exposure, if necessary. By taking advantage of the exposure latitude of the film, you can use ½ to 1 stop less than the exposure determined by using the ASA speed of the film and still process the film normally.

PROCESSING BLACK-AND-WHITE FILM

For best results, develop your film as recommended. Underdevelopment reduces negative contrast and causes loss of shadow detail. Overdevelopment increases contrast and graininess, reduces sharpness, and can block up highlights, making the negatives hard to print.

If you process your films yourself, follow the processing recommendations in the film instruction sheet. You'll also find helpful processing information in the KODAK Darkroom DATAGUIDE (R-20) and in the photo book KODAK Films—Color and Black-and-White (AF-1). Both Kodak publications are available from your photo dealer.

MARTY TAYLOR

Very dim light requires extremely high-speed film. Under a 40-watt bulb at night, KODAK ROYAL-X Pan Film— ASA 1250, 1/30 sec f/2.8

JOHN MENIHAN

Taking action pictures in dim light requires an extremely high-speed film, such as KODAK 2475 Recording Film (ESTAR-AH Base)—ASA 1000, 1/125 sec f/2.5.

Underexposing and push-processing allowed the photographer to use a shutter speed fast enough to slow the action of this nighttime motorcycle race. TRI-X Pan Film push-processed 1 stop, 1/250 sec f/1.8

Push-Processing KODAK Black-and-White Film

For some picture-taking situations in which you just don't have enough film speed, you may have to underexpose and push-process the film. Although some quality is lost when you under-expose and push-process your black-and-white film, you may be willing to accept the slight loss in shadow detail and image quality to get a picture that would otherwise be impractical or im-possible. By increasing development

time, you can obtain acceptable qual-ity in *most* black-and-white pictures that have been underexposed by 1 stop. (The amount by which you can underexpose will depend on the con-trast of the scene. See the last para-graph on page 77.) For example, you can expose KODAK TRI-X Pan Film at 800 instead of its rated speed of ASA 400. This doesn't mean that you have actually increased film speed. The speed of black-and-white film is not changed significantly when you

76

TRI-X Pan Film—ASA 400, 1/30 sec f/4, normal processing

TRI-X Pan Film—Film Speed Number 800, 1/30 sec f/5.6, push-processed 1 stop with a 50 percent increase in development time

alter exposure and increase development. As the pictures above illustrate, push-processing improves the quality of underexposed pictures in some respects but does not compensate fully for the loss in quality resulting from underexposure.

To push-process your black-and-white film when you have underexposed it by 1 stop, increase the development time recommended on the film instruction sheet by 50 percent. This is only a general rule, because the limit for push-processing varies according to the film and developer combination you use. For push-processing Kodak films, you can use the developers recommended on the film instruction sheet, *except* KODAK MICRODOL-X Developer. If the film doesn't have an instruction sheet, you can find the recommended developing time in either publication mentioned on page 75. Or write to Eastman Kodak Company, Photo Information, Department 841B, 343 State Street, Rochester, New York 14650.

Black-and-white negatives that have been underexposed and push-processed have increased contrast and graininess overall and increased density in most of the negative *except underexposed shadow areas.* To get acceptable contrast in your prints, you'll want to use a lower-contrast printing paper than you'd use with normally processed negatives. The prints will probably have poor shadow detail, but they should show good detail in the highlights and middle tones.

The degree to which you can underexpose your negatives and still produce acceptable prints depends to a large extent on scene contrast. The technique of underexposure and push-processing is not practical for high-contrast scenes because picture contrast will be increased to an unacceptable level. However, you can use this technique with low-contrast and normal-contrast scenes. Underexposure of normal-contrast scenes by more than 1 stop, with push-processing, will usually result in an excessive reduction in quality. If necessary, you can underexpose low-contrast scenes by 2 stops and obtain acceptable picture quality by increasing development time 50 percent. Be sure there is no important shadow detail present in the scene, since that detail will be lost because of too much underexposure.

Picture-taking is as simple or challenging as you want to make it. To make an outstanding photograph, it's often necessary to achieve the best balance of the many photographic principles involved. Under adverse conditions, it's sometimes desirable to compromise part of the picture-making process, such as exposure and development, to get the best possible picture under the circumstances.

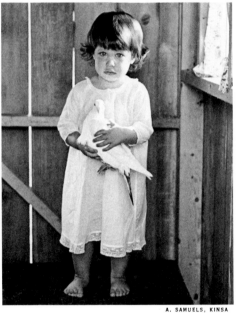

A. SAMUELS, KINSA

KODAK TRI-X Pan Film

SOME IMPORTANT POINTS TO REMEMBER

Color Films

- For taking pictures in daylight illumination, use Daylight film. You can also use Tungsten film with a No. 85B filter over your camera lens.

- To make natural-looking pictures in tungsten illumination, use Tungsten film. You can use Daylight film, but your pictures will have a yellow-red cast.

- For outdoor pictures at night, you can use either Tungsten or Daylight film.

- For pictures in fluorescent light without filters, Daylight film gives the best results, although the pictures appear greenish.

- When you have a combination of light sources in the same scene, use the type of film recommended for the predominant light source.

- You can use the KODAK Special Processing Envelope, ESP-1, to double the film speed of high speed KODAK EKTACHROME Films in the 120 and 135 sizes.

Black-and-White Films

- Use correct exposure and normal processing for the best quality in most pictures.

- In situations which require underexposure to get a picture, you can get acceptable quality with black-and-white films when you underexpose by 1 stop and push-process the film by increasing the developing time 50 percent. (KODAK MICRODOL-X Developer is not recommended for push-processing.)

Cut out the exposure table below and fold where indicated. It will fit in your shirt pocket, purse, or camera bag so that when you take pictures you'll have the exposure information handy to use.

Cut along this line.

SUGGESTED EXPOSURES FOR KODAK FILMS

Picture Subject	KODACHROME 64 (Daylight) EKTACHROME 64 (Daylight) KODACOLOR II	EKTACHROME 200 160 (Tungsten)—normal processing VERICHROME Pan PLUS-X Pan	EKTACHROME 400 (Daylight)—normal processing EKTACHROME 200 (Daylight) and 160 (Tungsten)—with ESP-1 Processing KODACOLOR 400 TRI-X Pan	EKTACHROME 400 (Daylight)—with ESP-1 Processing
INDOORS IN PUBLIC PLACES				
Basketball, hockey, bowling	1/30 sec f/2	1/60 sec f/2	1/125 sec f/2	1/125 sec f/2.8
Boxing, wrestling	1/60 sec f/2	1/125 sec f/2	1/250 sec f/2	1/250 sec f/2.8
Stage shows: Average	1/30 sec f/2	1/60 sec f/2.8	1/60 sec f/2.8	1/125 sec f/2.8
Stage shows: Bright	1/60 sec f/2.8	1/60 sec f/4	1/60 sec f/4	1/250 sec f/4
Circuses: Floodlighted acts	1/30 sec f/2	1/60 sec f/2.8	1/125 sec f/2.8	1/125 sec f/2.8
Spotlighted acts (carbon-arc)	1/30 sec f/2.8	1/125 sec f/2.8	1/125 sec f/2.8	1/250 sec f/4
Ice shows: Floodlighted acts	1/30 sec f/2.8	1/60 sec f/2.8	1/125 sec f/2.8	1/125 sec f/2.8
Spotlighted acts (carbon-arc)	1/60 sec f/2.8	1/125 sec f/2.8	1/125 sec f/2.8	1/250 sec f/4
Interiors with bright fluorescent light	1/30 sec f/2.8	1/60 sec f/4	1/125 sec f/4	1/250 sec f/5.6
School—stage and auditorium	—	1/15 sec f/2	1/30 sec f/2	1/30 sec f/2.8
Swimming pool—tungsten light indoors (above water)	1/15 sec f/2	1/30 sec f/2.8	1/60 sec f/2.8	1/60 sec f/2.8
Church interiors—tungsten light	1 sec f/5.6	1/30 sec f/2.8	1/60 sec f/2.8	1/60 sec f/2.8
Stained-glass windows, daytime—photographed from inside	Use 3 stops more exposure than for the outdoor lighting conditions.			
Glassware in windows, daytime—photographed from inside	Use 1 stop more exposure than for the outdoor lighting conditions.			

- For color pictures, use Tungsten film. You can use Daylight film, but your pictures will look yellow-red.
- For color pictures, use Daylight film, or Tungsten film with No. 85B filter and 1 stop more exposure.
- For color pictures, use either Daylight or Tungsten film.

*With KODACHROME 25 Film (Daylight), increase exposure by 1 stop.
†When lighting is provided by mercury-vapor lamps, use Daylight film.

Fold back here.

SUGGESTED EXPOSURES FOR KODAK FILMS

Picture Subject	KODACHROME 64 (Daylight) EKTACHROME 64 (Daylight) KODACOLOR II	EKTACHROME 200 160 (Tungsten)—normal processing VERICHROME Pan PLUS-X Pan	EKTACHROME 400 (Daylight)—normal processing EKTACHROME 200 (Daylight) and 160 (Tungsten)—with ESP-1 Processing KODACOLOR 400 TRI-X Pan	EKTACHROME 400 (Daylight)—with ESP-1 Processing
AT HOME				
Home interiors at night: Areas with bright light	1/15 sec f/2	1/30 sec f/2	1/30 sec f/2.8	1/30 sec f/4
Areas with average light	1/4 sec f/2.8	1/15 sec f/2	1/30 sec f/2	1/30 sec f/2.8
Candlelighted close-ups	1/4 sec f/2	1/8 sec f/2	1/15 sec f/2	1/30 sec f/2
Indoor and outdoor holiday lighting at night, Christmas trees	1 sec f/4	1 sec f/5.6	1 sec f/2	1/30 sec f/2
OUTDOORS AT NIGHT				
Brightly lighted downtown street scenes (wet streets add interesting reflections)	1/30 sec f/2	1/30 sec f/2.8	1/60 sec f/2.8	1/60 sec f/2
Brightly lighted nightclub or theatre districts—Las Vegas or Times Square	1/30 sec f/2.8	1/60 sec f/4	1/60 sec f/2.8	1/125 sec f/2.8
Neon signs and other lighted signs	1/30 sec f/2.8	1/60 sec f/4	1/125 sec f/2.8	1/125 sec f/5.6
Store windows	1/30 sec f/2.8	1/60 sec f/4	1/60 sec f/4	1/60 sec f/5.6
Floodlighted buildings, fountains, monuments	1 sec f/4	1 sec f/5.6	1 sec f/2.8	1 sec f/2
Skyline—distant view of lighted buildings at night	4 sec f/2.8	4 sec f/4	4 sec f/5.6	1/125 sec f/5.6
Skyline—10 minutes after sunset	1/30 sec f/4	1/60 sec f/4	1/60 sec f/5.6	1/60 sec f/2.8
Fairs, amusement parks	1/15 sec f/2	1/30 sec f/2	1/30 sec f/2.8	1/60 sec f/5.6
Fireworks—displays on the ground	1/30 sec f/2.8	1/30 sec f/4	1/60 sec f/4	1/60 sec f/5.6
Fireworks—aerial displays (Keep shutter open on Bulb or Time for several bursts)	f/8	f/11	f/16	f/22
Burning buildings, campfires, bonfires	1/30 sec f/2.8	1/30 sec f/4	1/30 sec f/4	1/60 sec f/5.6
Night football, baseball, racetrack‡	1/30 sec f/2.8	1/60 sec f/2.8	1/125 sec f/2.8	1/250 sec f/2.8
Niagara Falls: White lights	15 sec f/5.6	8 sec f/5.6	4 sec f/5.6	4 sec f/8
Light-colored lights	30 sec f/5.6	15 sec f/5.6	8 sec f/5.6	4 sec f/5.6
Dark-colored lights	30 sec f/4	30 sec f/5.6	15 sec f/5.6	8 sec f/5.6

ANSWERS TO YOUR QUESTIONS

*If you have specific questions about taking existing-light pictures,
write to Eastman Kodak Company, Photo Information, Department 841,
343 State Street, Rochester, New York 14650.*

EXISTING-LIGHT PICTURE-TAKING TIPS

- Focus carefully, because depth of field is shallow when you use large lens openings.
- Hold your camera steady and carefully press the shutter release to take the picture.
- Use a camera support for exposure times longer than $1/30$ second.
- Take along a flashlight so that you can see to make your camera settings in dim light.
- The exposures suggested in the tables are approximate. For especially important pictures, bracket your exposure by taking one picture at 1 stop more than the suggested exposure, one picture at the suggested exposure, and another at 1 stop less exposure.

Exposures for Your Own Specific Subjects

Subject	Film	Exposure

NOTES

80